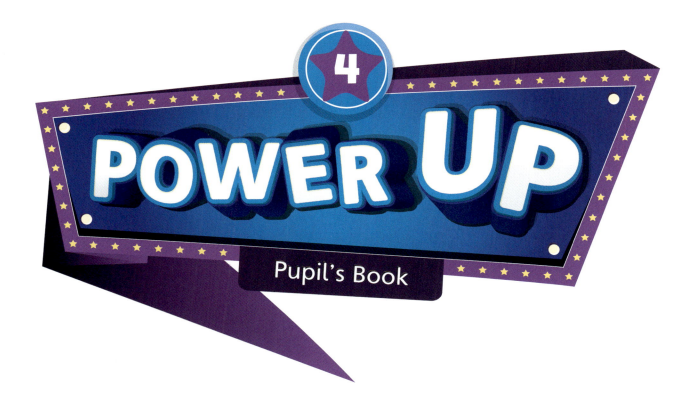

Caroline Nixon & Michael Tomlinson

Map of the book

		Vocabulary	Grammar	Cross-curricular	Literature	Assessment
	Meet Diversicus Page 4	Main character names Describing people	Revision of Level 3			
1	**This year's trip** Mission: Prepare a holiday planner for this school year Page 6	Months and ordinal numbers Journeys Sounds and spelling: stress in months vocabulary	**might/may** *It might be hot.* *You may need a strong pair of boots.* **Indefinite pronouns** *everywhere, somewhere, anywhere, nowhere; everyone, someone, anyone, no-one; everything, something, anything, nothing*	*What's the climate like?* Learn about climates and climate zones The Arabian Desert	*The lion of the seas* A children's encyclopedia entry Social and emotional skill: Self-confidence and bravery	A2 Flyers Reading and Writing Part 2
2	**Our beautiful planet** Mission: Write an explorer's expedition diary Page 18	The natural world Animals Sounds and spelling: silent *e*	**Past simple review: regular and irregular verbs; ago** *We got here a week ago.* *We didn't visit Uluru.* *Did you go away last month?* **too and enough** *There's too much plastic.* *There isn't enough water.*	*Save our world* Learn about endangered animals Animals in Australia	*When Dad lost his glasses* A poem Social and emotional skill: Showing awareness of how others feel	A2 Flyers Listening Part 2
3	**Let's celebrate!** Mission: Have a class quiz in teams Page 30	Competitions Music and festivals Sounds and spelling: *b* and *v*	**Present perfect for experience** *Have you ever eaten black beans?* *Have you ever danced samba?* **Present perfect with just, already, yet** *I've already taken more than 100 photos.* *I haven't seen the pyramids yet.* *We've just finished in Brazil.*	*Making music history* Learn about the history of musical instruments Brazilian carnival music	*The local football hero* A real-life story Social and emotional skill: Resilience and perseverance	A2 Flyers Listening Part 3
	Review Units 1–3					
4	**Time of our lives** Mission: Write a chain story about a mystery Page 44	Verbs for offers, promises and requests Telling the time Sounds and spelling: alternative spellings for *ee*	**Past continuous** *While I was cleaning my bike, my sister was watching TV.* *I was getting hot when Mum came out.* **Present perfect with since/ for** *We've been here since five past four.* *We've been here for a quarter of an hour.*	*Time zones* Learn about time zones New Year celebrations around the world	*The legend of Mother Mountain* A legend Social and emotional skill: Understanding how actions can affect the environment	A2 Flyers Listening Part 4

		Vocabulary	Grammar	Cross-curricular	Literature	Assessment
5	**Let it snow!** Mission: Prepare a TV weather report Page 56	Seasons and weather In winter Sounds and spelling: revision of *-er*, *-ar* and *-or* endings	**will/won't** *I'll water their garden.* *We won't talk about football.* **Conjunctions: *so* and *because*** *The weather's really cold, so we have to wear warm clothes.* *Today we couldn't go skiing because it was foggy.*	*Spring, summer, autumn, winter* Learn about why we have seasons Climate in Argentina	*Tomás and the snowman* A real-life story Social and emotional skill: Showing remorse	A2 Flyers Speaking Part 2
6	**Working together** Mission: Invent something to help with a job Page 68	Jobs World of work Sounds and spelling: stress in compound nouns	**Tag questions** *You eat everything, don't you?* *You can cycle, can't you?* **Short questions** *'I didn't go to the bank on Friday morning.' 'Didn't you?'* *'It was my twin brother.' 'Was it?'*	*Inventions and robotics* Learn about inventions and robotics South Korean inventions	*Buddie and Seo-joon's adventure* A science-fiction script Social and emotional skill: Friendship	A2 Flyers Reading and Writing Part 4
	Review Units 4–6					
7	**Then and now** Mission: Create an encyclopedia entry Page 82	Things in the home Adjectives to describe objects Sounds and spelling: *j* spelling	**Past participles** *seen, found, driven, ridden, taken, broken, gone, left, tried, forgotten, put, stood, fallen, cut* **be used for/to** *It was used for cooking food.* *It was used to cook food.*	*Time machines* Learn about the evolution of objects The pyramids of Ancient Egypt	*The boy king* A historical fiction story Social and emotional skill: Taking a different perspective	A2 Flyers Reading and Writing Part 5
8	**Space travel** Mission: Plan a space mission Page 94	In space Adventure words Sounds and spelling: *s* + consonant(s)	**will and going to** *Spaceships will improve.* *Are you going to watch space films?* **Review of past tenses** *Ivan landed his rocket on the new planet. He was turning off his engine when he heard a strange noise.*	*Preparing for Mars* Learn about space exploration An Italian astronaut at the ISS	*The space blog* A science-fiction story Social and emotional skill: Managing own emotions	A2 Flyers Reading and Writing Part 3
9	**Great bakers** Mission: Take part in a cooking competition Page 106	Mealtimes and snacks Cooking Sounds and spelling: *sh*	**It smells/tastes/looks/feels/sounds like …** *I wanted to know what it tasted like.* *It felt like dry grass.* *It smelt like carrot cake.* *It looked like a nest.* *It sounded like someone playing an electric guitar.* **make somebody + adjective** *The smell's making me hungry.*	*How chocolate is made* Learn about chocolate production Traditional food in the UK	*The gingerbread girl's adventure* A fairy tale adaptation Social and emotional skill: Being passionate about what you do	A2 Flyers Reading and Writing Part 6
	Review Units 7–9					
	Grammar reference page 120					

Meet Diversicus

1 🎧 1.02 **Listen. Who speaks in this part of the director's film?**

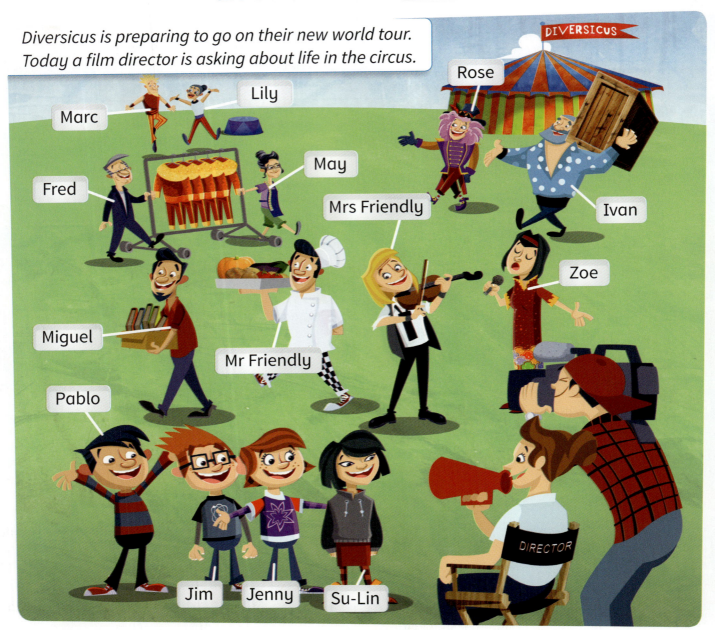

Diversicus is preparing to go on their new world tour. Today a film director is asking about life in the circus.

2 🎧 1.03 **Who says it? Listen and say the name.**

3 Play the describing game.

(Lily.) She's an acrobat. She's Pablo's mum. She's Marc's sister.

Describing people

4 Listen and say *yes* or *no*.

This year's trip

 Watch the video. Ask and answer.

What do you do in the school holidays?
Where would you like to go on a trip?

mission Prepare a holiday planner for this school year

In this unit I will:

1. Prepare a year planner.
2. Suggest and discuss options for different holidays.
3. Plan my holidays with a partner.
★ Present our holiday planner to the class.

Vocabulary 1

1 🎧 1.06 **Listen. Which countries do they talk about?**

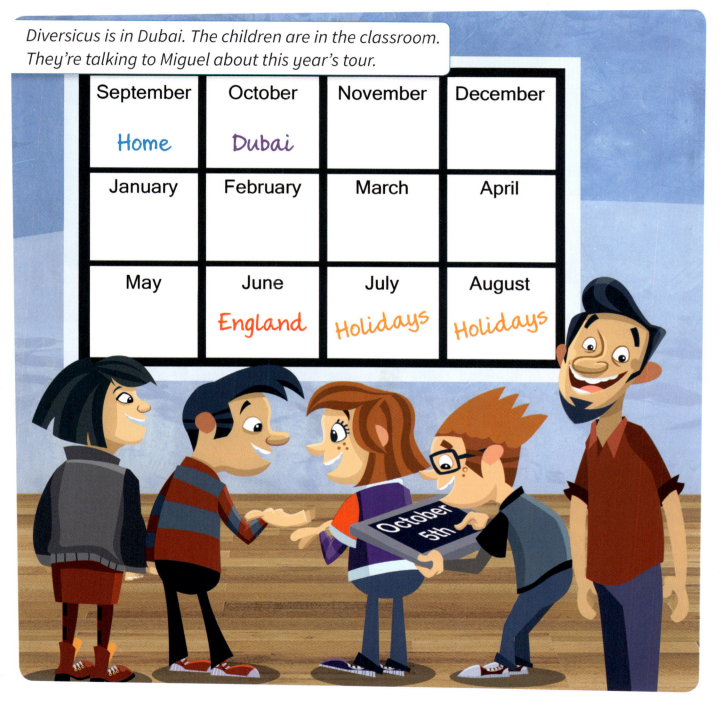

Diversicus is in Dubai. The children are in the classroom. They're talking to Miguel about this year's tour.

September	October	November	December
Home	Dubai		
January	February	March	April
May	June	July	August
	England	Holidays	Holidays

2 🎧 1.07 ▶ **Say the chant.**

3 **Tell your friend about something that happens in each month.**

In January, it's cold. I wear a coat.

In February, it's my sister's birthday.

Months and ordinal numbers 7

1 🎧 1.09 **Listen and say the number.**

Language practice 1

1 Describe the holiday photo. Then read the message.

Hi Emma! I can't wait for you to come next August! You might need to bring lots of different things because we aren't sure what we're going to do when you're here. It might be hot and Mum loves going to the beach, so you may need a beach towel and your swimsuit. Dad prefers to go camping in the mountains, so you may need a pair of strong boots. It might be cold in the mountains, so you might need a warm coat, too. I don't mind what we do, because I enjoy going to the beach and I love camping. So, we might go to the mountains or we might go to the beach, but I'm sure we're going to have a lot of fun together.

🎧 1.10 Grammar spotlight

It **might** be hot.   You **may** need a pair of strong boots.

2 Read the message to Emma again and complete the sentences. Use 1, 2, 3 or 4 words.

1. Emma _____ and towel for the beach.
2. In the mountains, the weather _____.
3. Emma _____ a pair of strong boots for camping in the mountains.
4. She might need a _____ because it's cold in the mountains.
5. They _____ to the mountains or the beach.

3 Imagine you're going to go camping or to the beach or to the sports centre. Say what you may or might do or see.

> I'm going to go to the beach. I might make a sandcastle.

 STAGE 1

Prepare your year planner.
- Put family and school dates on your planner. Discuss with a partner.

> What's happening in January?

> It's my grandma's birthday. It's on 15th January. We might have a party.

> We may have a school sports day in June. Why don't you include that?

> That's a good idea. Thanks.

My mission diary
Activity Book page 6

might/may

Vocabulary 2 and song

1 🎧 1.11 ▶ **Listen and match. Then sing the song.**

We're all going on a journey.
We're all going on a journey. (x2)
We're in the car on the ¹**motorway**,
Giving Frank a lift to the station. (x2)
Chorus
I see a ²**taxi** on the road and there's lots of ³**traffic**.
I see an ⁴**ambulance** and a ⁵**bicycle**. (x2)
Chorus
There's my train at the ⁶**railway** station.
There are ⁷**passengers** on the ⁸**platform**. (x2)
Chorus (x2)

2 🎧 1.13 📝 **Listen and write the words.**

3 **Play a game with a partner. Guess the word.**

It's when there are a lot of cars and lorries on the road.

Traffic.

How do you usually get to school?

10 Journeys

Language practice 2

1 🎧 1.14 Listen. Why is the shopping centre in Dubai special?

2 Copy and complete the grammar box. Listen and check.

🎧 1.15 Grammar spotlight

	all	+	-/?	-
	every	some	any	no
Where	everywhere	somewhere	anywhere	nowhere
Thing				
One				

3 Ask and answer.

QUICK QUIZ

1. Do you know anyone who … ?
2. Is there anywhere near here you can … ?
3. Can you tell me anything about … ?
4. Is there anyone in your family who … ?

Do you know anyone who lives in Dubai?

No, I don't.

mission STAGE 2

Suggest and discuss options for different holidays.
- Work with your Mission partner. Compare your year planners.
- Find dates when you're both free.
- Discuss and choose holidays together.

We're both free the first weekend in December. Shall we go skiing?

I think everyone might have the same idea, so it might be very busy.

Let's go on a bicycle trip before Easter!

That's a great idea! I love cycling!

My mission diary
Activity Book page 6

Indefinite pronouns

Cross-curricular

What's the climate like?

1 ▶ Watch the video.

2 Is the weather in your country the same all year?

3 🎧 1.16 Listen and read. Match the photos to the climate zones.

Why are there deserts in some countries and rainforests in other countries? It's always very cold at the North Pole and South Pole, even in summer. Why isn't it very cold all year where you live? Different places have different climates. Climate describes the usual weather of a place over many years and it influences the plants and animals that we find there. There are three main climate zones: **polar**, **temperate** and **tropical**.

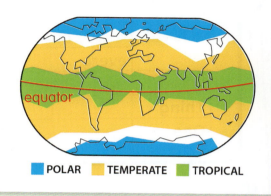

POLAR   TEMPERATE   TROPICAL

a

b

c

Polar climates are cold all year and there is always snow and ice. In winter the temperatures can be as low as -50°C and it's dark all the time. In summer there is sun nearly all day, but it's very weak, so it's still cold.

Temperate climates usually have winters that aren't very cold and summers that aren't very hot. Countries in the temperate climate zone have four seasons: winter, spring, summer and autumn.

Tropical climates are hot and humid all year. Countries near the equator are in the tropical climate zone. They don't have four seasons: they only have rainy and dry seasons.

4 Read the text again and answer the questions.

1 Which climate zone has rainy and dry seasons? _____

2 When is it dark all day in the polar climate zone? _____

3 To see autumn, which climate zone should you visit? _____

12   Learn about climates and climate zones

Culture

5 🎧 1.17 **Listen and read. Answer the questions.**

A desert is a place with little or no rain. They can be cold, like Antarctica, but many of them are hot, like the Arabian Desert. During the day here, temperatures are over 40°C, but at night, it's very cold and temperatures can fall below 0°C.

In the past, most people who lived in the desert were nomads. Nomads don't have a permanent home. They travel across the desert and they

have large tents which keep them cool during the day and warm at night. Traditional clothes use light colours because they're cooler than dark colours. They're also long to protect people's arms and legs from the sun and the sand.

Now, there are cities in the deserts because there are more ways of keeping cool. Dubai, in the United Arab Emirates, is a modern, exciting city in the Arabian Desert. The temperature in August is over 45°C. How do people keep cool there? There are artificial islands, and also beaches, but when it gets too hot to be outside, people stay at home or go to the air-conditioned shopping centres.

1 How are your summer clothes different from the clothes in the photo? _____

2 Why do people in Dubai spend a lot of time inside? _____

3 Do you wish you lived in Dubai? Explain your reasons to a partner. _____

Fun fact!

The tallest building in the world, Burj Khalifa, is in Dubai. It's 828 metres tall and it contains flats, a hotel, a gym, offices and shops.

 STAGE 3

Plan your holidays.

- In pairs, choose dates and decide how you're going to travel for each holiday.

  Let's travel by train.   *It's quicker than going by car.*

- Decide what you need to pack for each holiday.

  We need to pack our bike helmets.   *Yes. We need to pack warm coats, too. It's cold in the mountains in March.*

- Write your final holiday plans in your year planner.

My mission diary
Activity Book page 6

Learn about the Arabian Desert   13

Literature

1 Answer the questions.

1 Look at the text. What type of book would you find it in? How do you know?

2 Read the title and the sub-headings. What do you think the text is about?

THE LION OF THE SEAS
🎧 1.18

Name: Ahmad Ibn Majid
Occupation: Sailor, writer and poet
Year of birth: Around 1430
Place of birth: Julfar
Year of death: Around 1500

Julfar Today
Today Julfar is called Ras Al Khaimah. Ras Al Khaimah is nearly two hours' journey by motorway from Dubai. When Ahmad Ibn Majid was a boy, it was an important port.

Early Life

Ahmad Ibn Majid was the son of a famous sailor and he loved the sea. He liked watching the boats coming and going and he enjoyed talking to anyone who arrived by sea. He wanted to be a sailor, too. His father taught him the art of navigation. Ahmad Ibn Majid was very brave and confident. When he was 17, he could navigate a ship by himself.

Ahmad Ibn Majid: The Sailor
He studied the stars carefully and their position helped him to navigate ships. Other sailors called him 'The Shooting Star'. Soon he could sail from Julfar to East Africa, India and to many other distant locations. He understood about winds and tides, and the effect of the moon on the tides, and he could navigate through the roughest seas.

Text type: A children's encyclopedia entry

Ahmad Ibn Majid: The Writer
The sea, however, was not his only interest. He liked writing, too. He wrote 40 books about the sea, the stars and sea routes. He also wrote poetry. Soon he was famous and everyone talked about him.

Vasco da Gama

Ahmad Ibn Majid and Vasco da Gama
Vasco da Gama, the famous Portuguese explorer, wanted to sail from Portugal to India, but no-one knew the sea route from Europe to India at that time.

Vasco da Gama asked Ahmad Ibn Majid to help him. With his help, Vasco da Gama found the Cape of Good Hope in South Africa, sailed across the Indian Ocean and reached India.

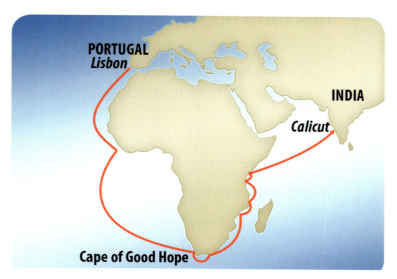

The route that Ahmad Ibn Majid helped Vasco da Gama to find

Why we remember him
Hundreds of years after he died, we still remember Ahmad Ibn Majid and his navigational skills. He's called 'The Lion of the Seas'. His books are in the National Library in Paris.

2 **Why do you think Ahmad Ibn Majid was called 'The Shooting Star' in his lifetime? Why do you think he's now called 'The Lion of the Seas'? Discuss in groups.**

3 **Think of a time when you were brave. What happened? Tell a partner.**

Social and emotional skill: Self-confidence and bravery

A2 Flyers

1 **Look at the picture and choose the correct answer.**

1 Who are the people?

A boy and his uncle. / A boy and his school friend. / Two brothers.

2 Where are they going?

To the beach. / To an office. / To the railway station.

2 **Now read the instructions. Are you right?** _____

> David is going with his Uncle Frank to the railway station today. David is asking Uncle Frank some questions about the journey.
> **What does Uncle Frank say?**

3 **Read and complete David's questions about the journey.**

1 _____ far is it to the station?
2 _____ are we going to get there?
3 _____ platform is our train on?
4 _____ there usually a lot of passengers?
5 _____ people take bicycles on a train?
6 If I'm hungry, _____ can we buy food?

4 **What kind of information does each answer need? Circle your answer.**

> a number   a time phrase   a yes/no answer   a place

5 **Now match David's questions with a reply.**

A In about five minutes. _____

B It's only about two miles from here. _____

C It's number one, near the drinks machine. _____

D Yes, they can – with a special ticket. _____

E There's a nice café opposite the ticket office. _____

F No, there aren't. October's a quiet month. _____

> Read all the choices before you choose an answer. In the exam there are two answers that you will not use.

Preparation for Reading and Writing Part 2

Review

mission in action!

Present your holiday planner to the class.

My mission diary — Activity Book page 6

- ★ Talk about your holidays.

> This year we're going to go on three holidays.

- ★ Explain where you and your partner are going to go on holiday and what you're going to do.

> We're going to go to the mountains in March. We're going to ride our bicycles every day.

- ★ Share the journey details and say what you're going to pack.

> We're going to leave on 24th March. We're going to go by train. We're going to take our bicycles, helmets and warm coats.

- ★ As a class, vote to choose your favourite holiday.

Can you remember?

1. In which month is Diversicus going to be in England?
2. What was the problem with Ivan's jacket?
3. What does Emma need to take with her on holiday?
4. What are the three main types of climate zones?
5. What's different about people who are nomads?
6. What name did sailors give to Ahmad Ibn Majid?

Unit consolidation

2 Our beautiful planet

1 ▶ **Watch the video. Ask and answer.**

What animals and plants can you see where you live?
What activities do you like doing outside?

mission Write an explorer's expedition diary

In this unit I will:

1. Describe my preparation and first day.
2. Describe what happened with some animals.
3. Write ideas about how to protect an endangered species.
★ Role play an interview with an explorer.

Vocabulary 1

1 **Listen. Where are the class going to camp? Name two places.**

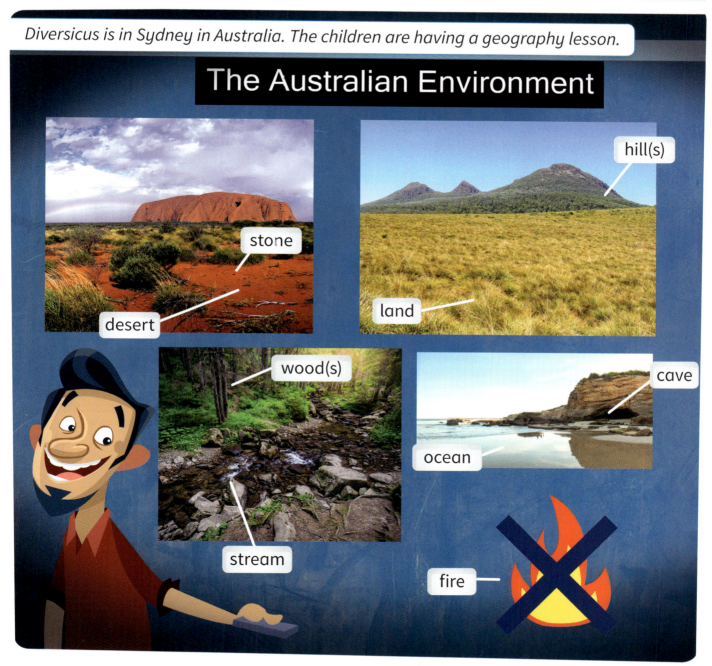

2 **Say the chant.**

3 **Play the spelling game.**

Number one: E-N-V-I-R-O-N-M-E-N-T.

1 environment

The natural world 19

Language practice 1

1 Look at the photo. What do you think Frank did on holiday?

2 Complete the text with the words from the box.

> ~~got~~   camped   stones   met   could   caves   visit

Well, here we are in Australia. We ¹_got_ here a week ago. On the first day, we ²_____ my dad's cousin and we explored some interesting ³_____ near a beach. We went on a boat with a glass floor, so we ⁴_____ see lots of amazing creatures.

Three days ago, we visited the Great Sandy Desert. We ⁵_____ in a big tent, but there were lots of ⁶_____ on the ground. We didn't ⁷_____ Uluru, the huge rock in the middle of Australia. Did you go away last month?

Frank

 Grammar spotlight

We **got** here a week **ago**.   We **didn't visit** Uluru.
Did you **go** away **last month**?

3 Play *Find someone who*. Ask and answer. Then tell the class.

mission STAGE 1

Choose where to explore and start your explorer's diary.
- Write about your trip preparation. Describe your first day.

> I packed my hat and a blanket. It gets cold at night. I arrived in the desert two days ago. We made a fire to keep warm.

- Talk to another explorer.

   When did you pack?   *I packed my suitcase two days ago.*

My mission diary
Activity Book page 18

Past simple review: regular and irregular verbs; *ago*   21

Vocabulary 2 and song

1 🎧 1.24 ▶ **Listen and match. Then sing the song.**

That was a [1]**dinosaur**,
But it's now extinct.
All there is on this dry land
Are its huge footprints.

[2]**Butterflies** and [3]**beetles**,
[4]**Eagles** in the air,
[5]**Camels** in the desert –
Creatures everywhere!

I'm a special [6]**tortoise**
With black [7]**swans** in the stream.
Look after our environment.
Don't let us be extinct!

**Chorus ... everywhere! ...
Creatures everywhere!**

I'm just an [8]**octopus**
Living in the sea.
Keep the ocean clean.
Don't let us be extinct!

**Chorus ... everywhere! ...
Creatures everywhere! (x2)**

2 📝 **Read and guess. Then write a description of a creature.**

This creature is an insect. It's usually small and beautiful. It's got four wings and six legs. It likes flying around flowers.

3 **Play the definition guessing game. Use your description from Activity 2.**

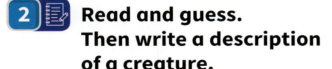
Let's talk about animals. Where do you see animals in your town?

22 Animals

Language practice 2

1 **Look at the pictures. What are the problems? Listen and check.**

Grammar spotlight

There's **too much** plastic. There are **too many** cars. The land is **too** dry.
There isn't **enough** water. There aren't **enough** trees. The air isn't clean **enough**.

2 Look and write sentences with *too* and *enough*.

> I think the air in cities is too dirty.

3 Ask and answer.

What do you do too much? What don't you do enough?
What have you got too much/many of? What haven't you got enough of?

> I don't tidy my bedroom enough.

> I've got too many old toys.

 **STAGE 2**

Describe what happened with some animals.
- Write about your day and tell a story about some animals.
- Discuss in groups.

> How was your day?

> I walked too near a snake. It was scary.

My mission diary
Activity Book page 18

too and *enough*

Cross-curricular

Save our world

1 Watch the video.

2 Listen and read. Answer the questions.

About 65 million years ago, Earth lost half of all its animals. Many people believe that a meteorite hit the planet and this caused the **extinction** of so many animals. Extinction happens when the last member of a species dies. Dinosaurs probably became extinct because of this natural disaster, but other animals are now extinct because of humans. One example is the dodo. Dodos lived on an island. When humans arrived, they hunted the birds and their dogs ate the dodos' eggs. Soon there were no more dodos.

dinosaurs   dodo

Today, we try harder to protect animals, but many are still **endangered**. This means that there aren't many of them alive, so they might become extinct in the future.

The list of endangered animals is very long and it includes polar bears, gorillas, rhinos and elephants.

polar bear   rhino

Animals become endangered for many reasons. Pollution and climate change are serious problems for all living things, but there are other reasons why so many animals are endangered. Hunters kill animals for their beautiful fur and some even kill them for sport. Humans cut down forests and change rivers to build cities and roads. This changes the animals' habitats and the animals lose their homes and food. These actions put animals in danger of extinction. We must remember that we share our planet. It doesn't belong to us.

1 What's the difference between extinct and endangered?

2 Why are animals endangered?

3 Look at the photos. How can we help? What other ways can you think of?

Learn about endangered animals

Culture

4 **Listen and read. Write *true* or *false*. Correct the false statements.**

Australia has lots of unusual animals and many of them only live there, and nowhere else, for example kangaroos and koalas. These are both **marsupials** – animals that carry their babies in a pouch.

Australia is also home to some very dangerous animals. It has more venomous species than any other country in the world. These include spiders, scorpions and snakes on land and jellyfish in the oceans.

The people in Australia work hard today to protect their unusual and special animals. They don't want more animals to become extinct, like the Tasmanian tiger. The last time anyone saw this amazing animal was nearly 100 years ago. It was a very strange animal. It had a dog's body, a wolf's head, a kangaroo's pouch and stripes like a tiger.

It walked on four legs, but it could also hop on two legs. It was the largest carnivorous marsupial on Earth. A **carnivorous** animal is an animal that eats meat. The Tasmanian tiger hunted at night. Unfortunately, Tasmanian tigers attacked sheep, so farmers hunted them and now experts believe that they're extinct.

1   Marsupials carry their babies in a pouch. _____
2   The Tasmanian tiger had a head like a dog. _____
3   It walked on four legs, but it could also hop like a kangaroo on two legs. _____
4   It hunted during the day. _____
5   People killed the animals because they had beautiful fur. _____
6   The Tasmanian tiger is endangered. _____

mission STAGE 3

Write ideas about how to protect an endangered animal.
- Do research about an endangered animal where you're exploring.
- Find out ways to protect this animal and write ideas.

> The Western Swamp Tortoise is endangered. We need to put more plants in the water where they live. Insects come when there are plants and the tortoises eat the insects.

My mission diary
Activity Book page 18

Learn about animals in Australia

Literature

1 What do you do when you lose something? Who helps you find it? Where do you think Dad finds his glasses in Amy's poem? Read and find out.

WHEN DAD LOST HIS GLASSES

On the first day of March we arrived on a plane
In Sydney, Australia, where there's not so much rain.
It was too hot for me and too hot for my dad
And Mum said, 'This weather's the hottest we've had!'

Yes, the sun was so high and the sky was so blue
And the air was so hot. Oh, what could we do?
'Let's go somewhere else,' I said, 'go somewhere cold,
To the lovely Blue Mountains where they say there is gold.'

So we drove in the car on the very next day
To the mountains that Mum said were not far away
And the caves that were dark and so quiet and cold –
Full of beautiful things, some new and some old.

26 Text type: A poem

We walked and we talked in these Jenolan Caves,
Mum, Dad and I, and our guide, Mr Graves.
'This is limestone,' he said, with his hand to the wall,
'And it makes all these shapes, so big and so tall.'

'Look at this,' said our guide, 'look up there, look at that!
Here's one like a hill! There's one like a hat!
Over time these things formed from the water that fell.
Do you like them? They've all got some stories to tell.'

We had a good time in these interesting caves
Until Dad said, 'My glasses! My gla- … Mr Graves!'
We looked for them here and we looked for them there
And Dad said, 'But when did I lose them? And where?'

But the torch on my helmet helped me to see,
So I looked in the dark that was all around me
And I said to my dad, 'They're on top of your head!'
He put them back on and his face was bright red.

2 **Answer the questions with a partner. Choose words from the box.**

> angry   surprised   tired   excited   pleased   interested   worried   thirsty

1. How did Amy and her parents feel when they arrived and it was very hot?
2. How did they feel when they saw the shapes in the caves?
3. How did Amy's dad feel when he couldn't find his glasses?
4. How did he feel when he realised they were on his head?

Social and emotional skill: Showing awareness of how others feel

A2 Flyers

1 Look at the picture. What kind of activities do you think the children did on their trip?

_____

2 Look at the notes. What kind of information is missing for each space?

> a noun (x 3)   a name   a number

School trip
Place: Ocean and _Desert_ World
1 Class: _____
2 Name of teacher: Mr _____
3 First day: fed the _____
4 Everyone had to: write a _____
5 Last day: children visited a _____

3 🎧 1.31 Complete the notes with the words in the box. Listen and check.

> cave   sharks   diary
> Taylor   6   Desert

School trip
Place: Ocean and _____ World
1 Class: _____
2 Name of teacher: Mr _____
3 First day: fed the _____
4 Everyone had to: write a _____
5 Last day: children visited a _____

4 🎧 1.32 Listen and write the surnames of these children on the trip.

1 Dan _____   2 Alice _____   3 Lily _____

> Make sure you know the letters of the alphabet and always check your spelling.

5 Practise spelling with a friend.

| 5 animal words | 5 surnames | 5 environment words |

Swan.   S-W-O …   No, try again!   S-W-A-N.   Yes! Well done!

Preparation for Listening Part 2

Review

mission in action!

Role play an interview with an explorer.

My mission diary
Activity Book page 18

★ Ask other explorers about their arrival at the camp and use your diary to answer.

What did you do on your first night?

★ Ask and answer about incidents with animals.

Did you see any interesting animals?

★ Ask about each explorer's animal research and give the ideas you wrote about how to protect an endangered animal.

Did you find out about any endangered animals? How can we help them?

Can you remember?

1. Which subject was Miguel teaching the children? _____
2. Which animal was outside Jenny's tent? _____
3. Where did Frank and his family go on their first day in Australia? _____
4. Name three animals that are endangered. _____
5. Why do people think Tasmanian tigers are extinct? _____
6. Who lost his glasses in the Jenolan Caves? _____

Unit consolidation

3 Let's celebrate!

1 ▶ **Watch the video. Ask and answer.**

Do you celebrate any festivals where you live?
What do you do to celebrate?

mission Have a class quiz in teams

In this unit I will:

1. Write questions about Diversicus.
2. Write quiz questions about experiences in my group.
3. Research a country's music and write quiz questions.
★ Take part in a quiz.

Vocabulary 1

1 Listen. Which country won the men's beach volleyball? Which country won the women's cycling road race?

Diversicus is in Brazil. This morning, Ivan and the children are on the beach.

team · score · match · prize · volleyball · Olympic Games in Brazil · stadium · puzzle · quiz · chess · race · winner

2 Say the chant.

3 Listen and say *yes* or *no*.

Competitions

Language practice 1

1 Look at the pictures. Talk about them.

2 Circle the words to complete the questions in the advert.

1 Have you ever **eaten**/**eat** black beans?
2 Have you ever **spent**/**spend** the day at the beach?
3 Have you ever **have**/**had** mango ice cream?
4 Have you ever **swum**/**swim** in the sea?
5 Have you ever **drink**/**drunk** juice out of a coconut?
6 Have you ever **go**/**gone** to the market to buy food?
7 Have you ever **danced**/**dance** samba?
8 Have you ever **be**/**been** to a carnival?

If you have said **No** to any of these, then come to Brazil! You can do all of these and more. Book your ticket today!

🎧 1.38 Grammar spotlight

Have you ever **eaten** black beans?   **Have** you ever **danced** samba?

3 Ask and answer the questions in the advert. Write about your friend.

> João has eaten black beans, but he hasn't …

 **STAGE 1**

Write questions about Diversicus.

- In groups, write three Yes/No questions and answers about the characters.
  Use the present perfect.

Have the Friendly family been to Australia?
a Yes, they have.
b No, they haven't.

Has Ivan pulled a plane?
a Yes, he has.
b No, he hasn't.

Activity Book page 30

Present perfect for experience

Vocabulary 2 and song

1 🎧 1.39 ▶ Listen and match. Then sing the song and do the actions.

At the [1]**festival**,
[2]**Musicians** who [3]**rock**
Join in the music –
Hip-hop or [4]**pop**!
At the festival!

At the [5]**concert**
Wave your [6]**flags**!
Play your [7]**instruments**!
Don't be sad!
At the concert!

[8]**Whistle** a [9]**tune**!
Hit the [10]**drums**!
Let's meet on [11]**stage**
With our mums!
At the concert!

Lily can swing
To Mum's [12]**violin**.
Zoe can sing
With Su-Lin.

2 🎧 1.41 📝 Listen and write the words.

3 Play the memory game.

Mrs Friendly's playing the guitar.

No, she isn't. She's playing the violin.

Let's talk about music. What type of music do you like?

34 Music and festivals

Language practice 2

1 🎧 2.02 **Listen and look. What does Jim want to see?**

Where?	Oct	Nov	Dec	Jan	Feb	Mar	Apr	May	Jun
Last year	Russia	China	Indonesia	India	Greece	Turkey	Spain	USA	Mexico
This year	Dubai	Australia	Brazil	?	?	?	?	?	?

🎧 2.03 **Grammar spotlight**

I've **already** taken more than 100 photos.

I haven't seen the pyramids **yet**.

We've **just** finished in Brazil.

2 **Where have they been? Ask and answer about Diversicus.**

Italy   South Korea   Greece   Turkey   Ecuador   Spain
Russia   Mexico   Portugal   Indonesia

Have they been to Russia yet?   Yes, they've already been there.

Have they been to Italy yet?   No, they haven't been there yet.

 **STAGE 2**

Write quiz questions about experiences in your group.

- Talk about your experiences and choose three.

   Has anyone ever been skiing?   Yes, I have. Let's choose that.

- For each experience, write three present perfect sentences about your group. Only one sentence is correct.

   1 Skiing
   a   Pablo has been skiing.
   b   Julia and Sam have been skiing.
   c   Everyone in our group has been skiing.

My mission diary
Activity Book page 30

Present perfect with *just, already, yet*   35

Cross-curricular

Making music history

 Watch the video.

 Listen and name the instruments.

 Listen and read. Then order the photos from the oldest instrument (1) to the most modern (4).

The guitar is one of the most popular musical instruments in the world. Many different cultures have played instruments like the guitar for over 3,000 years. The oldest instrument that we can see today comes from Ancient Egypt. You can see this guitar in a museum in Cairo. It belonged to a singer who sang for the Egyptian queen Hatshepsut. This type of guitar had a long neck and only three strings.

The lute is also an ancient instrument similar to a guitar, but it has a short neck and a body like half a pear. It usually had more strings than a guitar and they were in pairs. From 1100–1500, travelling singers and story tellers played the lute to accompany their songs.

Guitars sometimes had pairs of strings like the lute, but the guitar changed over time to use single strings. People used guitars with six single strings for the first time in the 1600s in Italy, but the most important change happened in the 1850s. The Spanish guitar maker Antonio Torres Jurado made the guitar's body bigger. His idea made the sound of the guitar louder and better. Most of today's classical guitars follow his design.

The first electric guitars appeared in the 1930s. The electric guitar has a solid body and can make many different sounds. We also find them in many different shapes and sizes. Some electric guitars don't look like guitars at all!

Learn about the history of musical instruments

Culture

4 Read the text. When and how do you listen to music? What music do people in your family like? What festivals with music are there in your country?

Music is all around us. We can hear it everywhere. We can also take it with us wherever we go, but that wasn't possible until the 1980s. Now we have our favourite music on our phones and on our computers. Headphones let us listen to our music on the bus or in the car. We can hear it, but other people can't. This is good because not everyone likes the same kind of music! There are many styles of music. Some people like classical music and others like folk, jazz or hip-hop.

Music is important in many cultures and different musical instruments are typical in different places. In many countries the drum is the most important instrument and you can see them in different shapes and sizes. Music is also very important at festival time in many countries.

5 Listen to Liliana talking about music at the Rio Carnival. Read and choose the correct words.

1. Brazil celebrates carnival in *February or March* / *December or January*.
2. Carnival happens *only in Rio de Janeiro* / *all over Brazil*.
3. People celebrate carnival *at home* / *in the streets*.
4. Samba music came from *Africa* / *America*.
5. Samba musicians use guitars and *trumpets* / *drums*.

6 Make your own Brazilian instruments. Use materials that you have at home or in class.

 STAGE 3

Research a country's music and write quiz questions.
- Choose a country and research its music.
- Write three quiz questions. Give three possible answers (only one of which is correct).

"Let's find out about music in …"

"Good idea!"

Activity Book page 30

Learn about Brazilian carnival music

Literature

1 Which sports people do you like? How do you think their life changed when they became famous?

🎧 2.07 THE LOCAL FOOTBALL HERO

My name is Rebeca and I'm 11. I'm from beautiful Brazil! But my family live in a poor area, and life isn't easy. My parents work hard so my brother and I can go to school, and we always come straight home after school to help with the housework. But I have a passion … football! And I want to tell you how football has changed my life.

My dad wanted my big brother to be a professional football player, but he didn't like training. I loved football and when I played I felt happy and I forgot about everything around me. My mum said, 'Football isn't for girls.' The boys at school didn't want to play with a girl either, but when they saw I was good, they picked me for their team.

One day a teacher told me about a football team just for girls. They were amazing. They told me that they were preparing for a competition in March. I really wanted to be part of the team and I decided to try my hardest.

38 | Text type: A real-life story

When I told my dad and brother, they were very happy. My mum still didn't like the idea. 'It isn't going to be easy for you because football is a boy's sport,' she said. But she said nothing after that, and my dad and brother trained with me every day for six months. Finally, in February the coach told us which players were in the team for the competition. When I heard my name, I jumped in the air and I screamed with excitement.

Our team travelled to Rio de Janeiro in March and we won the competition – it was amazing! Since then we've won a lot more matches, but more importantly, I've made lots of new friends and I've become more confident about myself.

When I get older, I want to be a professional football player. Lots of my football idols have learnt English. For me, it's important to speak English just like them and study hard so I can travel round the world and talk to people from different countries. That's now my biggest dream in life.

2 Answer the questions.

1 How did football make Rebeca feel?
2 What sport or activity makes you feel the same as Rebeca? Why?

3 Rebeca practised a lot to achieve her dreams, even though it was difficult. Do you have a dream? Is it easy to achieve it?

Social and emotional skill: Resilience and perseverance

A2 Flyers

1 Look at the pictures. Where might you see these things?

> You might see a drum in a music shop.

violin

drum

puzzle book

2 Listen. Which object in Activity 1 is Aunt Helen talking about? How do you know?

3 What might you find in these places?

A

B

C

D

> Picture A – ball, grass …

4  Listen and match a picture A–D with each word in Activity 1. Which letter didn't you use? Why?

> In the exam, there are **two** extra pictures, but you will hear something about **all** of the pictures. Use the second listening to check your final choices.

Preparation for Listening Part 3

Review

mission in action!

Have a class quiz in teams.

- ★ In your group, think of a team name.
- ★ Ask the other teams your quiz questions.
- ★ The teams circle the correct letter for each question.
- ★ Change answer sheets. Count up the scores.

"We're The Samba Stars!"

My mission diary
Activity Book page 30

Can you remember?

1. What game were Ivan, Pablo and Jenny playing on the beach?
2. What hasn't Ivan lifted before?
3. Name three things you can do in Brazil.
4. Where's the oldest type of guitar from?
5. In which months does Brazil celebrate carnival?
6. Who didn't think Rebeca should play football?

Review — Units 1–3

1 Watch the video and do the quiz.

2 2.10 Copy the table. Listen to Katy and George and complete the birthdays. Then listen again and complete the notes.

Name	Birthday	What did they do on their last birthday?
Katy	14th April	went to _____ with her _____
George		played _____ in _____
Emma		went _____ in the _____
Michael		broke _____ in _____

3 Work with a partner. Play the game. Take it in turns.

- Student A: Choose two pictures for your partner. Say one thing that is the same about the two things.
- Student B: Say one thing that is different about the two things.

Swan and eagle! They can both fly.

A swan lives on water, but an eagle lives on land.

Consolidation of units 1–3

4 Read the interview. Then read and correct the sentences.

E Hi, David. I'm writing a quiz. Can I please ask you some questions? You may win a prize!
D Sure! Go ahead!
E Have you ever swum in a lake?
D No, I haven't. Everyone I know has swum in the sea, but no-one has swum in a lake.
E Have you ever been to a festival?
D No, I haven't – not yet! My mum says I'm not old enough to go.
E Have you ever sent a postcard?
D Yes, I've just sent one to my cousin to say thank you for looking after my tortoise. Postcards aren't too expensive, so I send them from everywhere I go on holiday.
E Have you ever been somewhere really hot, like a desert?
D No, I haven't. It's too hot for me there and I like having enough water to drink!
E Thanks, David! Hmm … I'm sorry, you only answered 'yes' to one question, so you aren't the winner.
D Oh no! I've never won a prize!

1 David has swum in a lake.

2 David doesn't know anyone who has swum in the sea.

3 David's mum thinks David is old enough to go to a festival.

4 David has sent only one postcard. He thinks they're too expensive.

5 David has been to a desert.

5 Now write your own interview for a friend. Think of six questions and then ask and answer.

- Write questions about transport, animals, music/festivals and competitions.
- Start your questions with: *Have you ever … ?*
- Write your questions. Ask your friend and write their answers.

Consolidation of units 1–3

4 Time of our lives

 Watch the video. Ask and answer.

Where can you see clocks?
Do you always get up and go to bed at the same time?

LA CANDELARIA

mission
Write a chain story about a mystery

In this unit I will:

1. Decide on the setting and characters for a story.
2. Describe a problem.
3. Describe how the problem is solved.
★ Finish and read the stories.

Vocabulary 1

1 **Listen. Why is Rose worried?**

2 🎧 2.12 ▶ **Say the chant.**

3 🎧 2.13 **Who says it? Listen and say the name.**

Verbs for offers, promises and requests

Language practice 1

1 What do you have to do before you can ride the bike in the photo?

2 Complete the text using the correct words from the list below.

Last weekend Mum ¹ <u>asked</u> my older sister and me to clean and repair our bikes. Both bikes had small holes in the tyres so we couldn't cycle to the park. While I ² _____ cleaning my bike, my sister was ³ _____ cartoons on TV! I was getting hot and angry when Mum came out to help me. She brought me some juice which I drank ⁴ _____ I was repairing the tyre. Mum and I were ready to go. We ⁵ _____ getting on our bikes when my sister ⁶ _____ out to join us. She couldn't come because her bike wasn't ready!

1	ask	asking	asked	**4** while	who	why
2	is	was	were	**5** are	was	were
3	watched	watching	watches	**6** came	come	comes

🎧 4.06 **Grammar spotlight**

<u>While</u> I was cleaning my bike, my sister was watching TV.

when Mum came out. I was getting hot

3 Choose words from your teacher's lists. Make sentences and act them out.

> You were hopping when you fell over.

mission STAGE 1

Plan your mystery story.
- In groups, choose your setting. Think about your characters.
- Choose a title. Give your plan to your teacher for another group.

> The story takes place in the colourful city Cartagena de Indias. Sally, Lily, Pedro and Marco are four friends who met while …
> Our title: What was Pedro doing at the Clock Tower?

My mission diary
Activity Book page 44

Past continuous

Vocabulary 2 and song

1 🎧 2.17 ▶ **Listen and match. Then sing the song.**

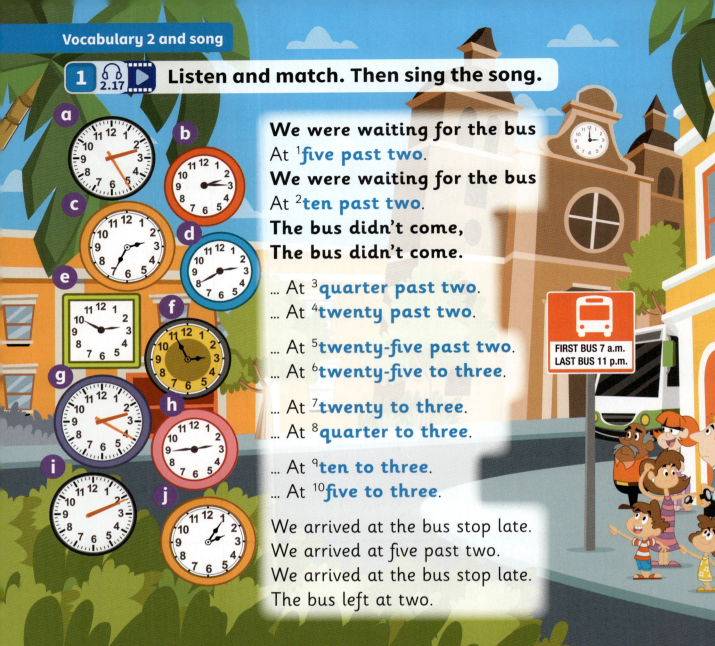

We were waiting for the bus
At ¹**five past two**.
We were waiting for the bus
At ²**ten past two**.
The bus didn't come,
The bus didn't come.

… At ³**quarter past two**.
… At ⁴**twenty past two**.
… At ⁵**twenty-five past two**.
… At ⁶**twenty-five to three**.
… At ⁷**twenty to three**.
… At ⁸**quarter to three**.
… At ⁹**ten to three**.
… At ¹⁰**five to three**.

We arrived at the bus stop late.
We arrived at five past two.
We arrived at the bus stop late.
The bus left at two.

2 **Write five questions about yesterday.**

in the morning   in the afternoon
in the evening   at night

1 What were you doing at twenty-five to eight in the morning?

2 What was your mum doing

3 Ask and answer your questions with a partner.

What were you doing at twenty-five to eight in the morning?

I was getting dressed.

How long does it take you to get to school? What time do you usually arrive?

Telling the time

Language practice 2

1 **Listen. What time does the bus usually arrive?**

Grammar spotlight

(We arrived at five past four.)   (Now it's twenty past four.)

We've been here **since** five past four.

We've been here **for** a quarter of an hour.

2 Write the questions.

1. How long / you / be / at this school?
2. How long / you / live / here?
3. How long / you / study / English?
4. How long / you / have / your shoes?
5. How long / you / know / your teacher?
6. How long / you / … ?

3 Ask and answer the questions from Activity 2 with a partner.

> How long have you been at this school?

> I've been here for four years.
> I've been here since I was five.

mission

Describe a problem for the mystery story.
- In groups, read the setting, characters and title of the story you have.
- Think of a problem and write the 'build-up' part of the story.
- Give the story to your teacher for another group.

> The four friends were going to meet at eleven o'clock.
> Sally, Lily and Marco arrived at eleven o'clock at the Barrio de Getsemaní, but Pedro …
> A little later, Sally said, 'How long have we waited for? We've …'
> 'What can we do now? Pedro doesn't have a phone,' said Lily.

My mission diary
Activity Book page 44

Present perfect with *since/for*

Cross-curricular

Time zones

1 Watch the video.

2 Listen and read. Answer the questions.

As Earth turns in space, the sun shines on only part of the planet. When it's day where you live, it's night time on the other side of the world. This means that when you're eating your breakfast, other children are going to bed. It's a different time in their country because the world has different **time zones**.

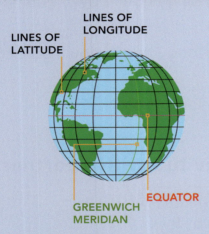

A map of the world has lots of lines on it. Lines of **latitude** go around Earth. They show us the distance from the **equator**, the line that goes round the middle. Lines of **longitude** go up and down, dividing Earth like pieces of an orange.

The **Greenwich Meridian** is a very important line of longitude which passes through London in the UK. It traditionally sets the time for all the clocks around the world. The time on this line of longitude is Greenwich Mean Time (GMT). If you live to the **east** of the Greenwich Meridian, it's later than in London. If you live to the **west**, it's earlier. Large countries like the USA have three or more time zones, but most countries have one, so the time is the same everywhere in that country. Before you phone a friend, check what time it is in their country. You might call them at 3.00 in the morning and no-one wants to talk then!

1   Explain the difference between lines of latitude and lines of longitude.

2   Is New York to the west or to the east of the Greenwich Meridian?

3   Is the time in New York earlier or later than GMT?

Learn about time zones

Culture

3 Look at the photos and read. What are they celebrating? What do the GMT labels mean?

GMT – 5 hours
New York, the USA

GMT + 2 hours
Athens, Greece

GMT + 10 hours
Sydney, Australia

It's 31st December, a special celebration in many parts of the world. It's a time when we hope for the future. Each country has its own traditions at this time.

4 🎧 2.22 Listen to the children talking about celebrations in their countries. Write *K* (*Ken*), *M* (*Maria*) or *D* (*Dom*).

1 _____ eats 12 pieces of fruit.
2 _____ has a party at the beach.
3 _____ might get money for singing.
4 _____ watches fireworks on the bridge.
5 _____ puts a vegetable on their door.
6 _____ puts an extra plate on the table.

5 How do you celebrate New Year? Talk with a partner.

6 Find out when and how people celebrate Chinese New Year. Use the internet to help you.

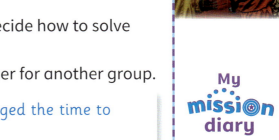

mission STAGE 3

Continue the story.

- In groups, read the 'build-up' part of the story and decide how to solve the problem.
- Write the 'resolution' and give the story to your teacher for another group.

Sally said, 'I know what happened! Pedro hasn't changed the time to Colombian time!'

'You're right. Let's go to the Clock Tower. I think he's there!' said Marco.

My mission diary
Activity Book page 44

Learn about New Year celebrations around the world

Literature

1 Look at the pictures. What is the setting for the story? Why do we need to protect this place? How can we do this?

THE LEGEND OF MOTHER MOUNTAIN

2.23

Somewhere deep in the rainforests and mountains of Colombia there's a very special woman. You may never see her, but she's there all the same. She wears a dress made of leaves. She's got no shoes on her feet and she has a ring of wild flowers on her head. Her name is Mother Mountain. Her job is to look after nature and the environment, and to make sure that no-one harms it. The animals of the rainforests and mountains love her. She's their friend, and they know that they're safe with her.

One day a man came to the forest to cut down some trees. As he was swinging his axe at a tree, Mother Mountain suddenly appeared from nowhere and caught his axe in her strong hands. The man turned and looked at her in amazement. 'Why have you come into the rainforest?' Mother Mountain asked. 'To cut wood to burn for our fires,' the man said. 'You can't cut down my trees,' Mother Mountain said. Slowly her green eyes turned red as she said:

'The environment is important for you and me!

Go to sleep now. Then wake up and see!'

Immediately the man fell to the ground in a deep sleep. The tree moved in the wind. It seemed to be saying 'Thank you, Mother Mountain.'

Text type: A legend

A few minutes later, another man came into the forest. He didn't see the man asleep on the ground, but he saw a bear. As he was getting ready to catch it with a net, Mother Mountain suddenly appeared from nowhere and caught the net in her strong hands. 'Why have you come into the forest?' she asked. 'To get meat for my children to eat,' the man said. 'You can't kill my animals,' Mother Mountain said. Slowly her green eyes turned red and she said:

'The environment is important for you and me!

Go to sleep now. Then wake up and see!'

The man fell to the ground in a deep sleep. The bear touched Mother Mountain and made a soft noise. It seemed to be saying 'Thank you, Mother Mountain.'

The two men slept for several hours. Then they woke up from their deep sleep and they looked round. They didn't see Mother Mountain. She wasn't there. They only saw how beautiful the forest and its animals were. They walked home together, promising never to cut down a tree or hurt an animal ever again.

2 Why are the men never going to cut down a tree or hurt an animal again?

3 Do you do anything to look after nature and natural places?

4 In groups of five, act out the story. Decide who's going to be Mother Mountain, the two men, the tree and the bear.

Social and emotional skill: Understanding how actions can affect the environment

A2 Flyers

1 Michael was doing one of these activities yesterday at 5 p.m. What are the different activities?

A

B

C

2 🎧 2.24 Listen and say the order you hear the activities.

3 🎧 2.25 Look at the pictures carefully. Then listen and read the question and the conversation. Answer the question.

A

B

C

Where was Mum waiting for Michael?

Michael: I left school late because Mr March told us to tidy the playground. Can we still go to the cinema?

Mum: Well, only if there's a later time for the film …

Michael: I can find out on my tablet. Yes! At eight o'clock.

Mum: OK, as it's Friday, but we need a bus back here to the bus station after the film. Let's look at the times.

Remember to choose your answer when each part of the conversation finishes. You always listen again so you can check your answer.

Review

mission in action!

Finish and read the stories.

My mission diary
Activity Book page 44

★ In groups, write the end of the story which you now have.

Sally, Lily and Marco arrived at the Clock Tower and they saw Pedro.
'Hi Pedro!' the friends said.
'Hi! I've waited for half an hour!' Pedro said.
'You haven't changed your watch to Colombian time!' Sally said. 'It's 12 o'clock here.'
'Oh no!' Pedro said. They all laughed. THE END.

★ Next, read the finished story to the whole class.

This story takes place …   The title of the story is …

★ Finally, as a class vote to choose your favourite story.

The best story is …

Can you remember?

1. Why was the Friendly family late for lunch at Diversicus? _____
2. What did Jim and Jenny need to study for? _____
3. Why did the girl have to repair her bike? _____
4. What's the name of the line that goes round the middle of our planet? _____
5. In which country do people eat 12 grapes at New Year? _____
6. What does Mother Mountain wear? _____

5 Let it snow!

 Watch the video. Ask and answer.

Does it snow where you live?
What do you like doing when the weather is cold?

mission Prepare a TV weather report

In this unit I will:

1. Research winter weather in a different country.
2. Draw a map with weather symbols.
3. Write some travel advice.
⭐ Act out a TV weather report.

Vocabulary 1

1 🎧 2.26 **Listen. In which months is the temperature usually coldest?**

Diversicus is in Patagonia in the south of Argentina. It's a cold, foggy day.

spring | summer | autumn | winter | fog | storm | warm | ice

2 🎧 2.27 ▶ **Say the chant.**

3 **Ask and answer questions about the weather where you live.**

- What's the weather like here in spring?
- It's warm and sunny, but there are sometimes storms.

Seasons and weather 57

Language practice 1

1 Look at the pictures. What are the children doing?

2 Read. Answer the questions.

HelpatHome - online

HelpatHome: Mr and Mrs Hill are old and they're part of our 'Help at Home' programme. Who can help?

Robert: I'll feed their cat.

Sarah: My brother and I will do their shopping for them.

Katy: I'll make them a sandwich.

Harry: I'll water their garden.

HelpatHome: Excellent. Who wants to sit and chat with them? And what time will you go?

George: Betty and I will sit and talk to them after school. We won't talk about football because Mrs Hill hates it.

1 Who'll feed their cat?

2 What'll Sarah and her brother do?

3 Will Katy make them some soup?

4 What'll Harry do?

5 Who'll chat with Mr and Mrs Hill?

6 What won't they talk about?

Grammar spotlight

I**'ll water** their garden.   We **won't talk** about football.   What time **will** you **go**?

3 How will you help? Write three sentences.

I'll tidy their bedroom.

mission STAGE 1

Research winter weather in a different country.
- In groups, choose a country that isn't your own.
- Research the weather in winter.

I think it's foggy and cold.

What's the weather like in Canada in winter?

My mission diary
Activity Book page 56

will/won't   59

Vocabulary 2 and song

1 **Listen and match. Then sing the song.**

My friend's made a ¹**snowman**.
I haven't got my ²**gloves**.
My hands are in my ³**pockets**.
I have to stand and watch.

He's ⁴**skiing** down the mountain.
She's riding on her ⁵**sledge**.
He's making lots of ⁶**snowballs**.
To throw them at his friend.

He's carrying his ⁷**snowboard**.
He's going to the top.
⁸**Snowboarding** isn't easy –
I hope that she can stop.

The temperature has dropped a lot.
They've put their ice skates on.
They're skating very fast now.
They're on the icy ⁹**pond**.

2  **Listen and write the words.**

3 **Play a miming game.**

What am I doing?

Yes, I am.

Are you throwing a snowball?

What do you like to do in winter?

In winter

Language practice 2

1  **Listen and choose the correct picture.**

1 What clothes do George and Grandpa talk about?

A  B  C

2 What have George and his parents decided to do tomorrow?

A  B  C

 Grammar spotlight

The weather's really cold, **so** we have to wear warm clothes.
Today we couldn't go skiing **because** it was foggy.

2 Match to make correct sentences. Write the sentences.

1 There was a bad storm, …   a because there was a lot of snow.
2 They were wearing warm clothes … b so we could go sledging.
3 It snowed heavily, …   c so we couldn't play in the park.

 **STAGE 2**

Draw a map with weather symbols.
- In groups, draw a map of the country you chose.
- Draw the weather symbols on your map for a day in winter.

> The weather in the north is foggy and cold because it's near the sea.

> It's snowy in the east because there are mountains.

Activity Book page 56

Conjunctions: *so* and *because*

Cross-curricular

Spring, summer, autumn, winter

1 Watch the video.

2 Listen and read. Why do some parts of the world have seasons?

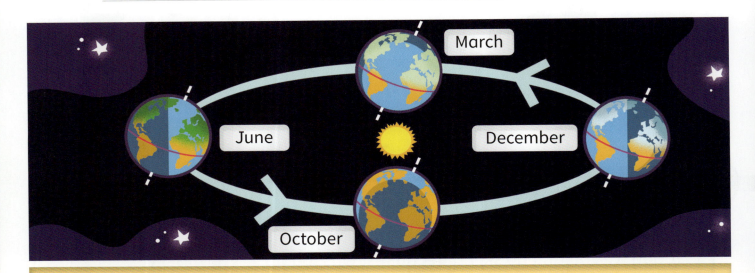

You know that the **equator** is an imaginary line that goes around Earth. It divides Earth into two **hemispheres**: the northern and southern hemispheres.

Earth's **axis** is another imaginary line. It passes through the centre of Earth between the North Pole and the South Pole.

You can see in the diagrams that Earth's axis isn't vertical. It **tilts** to one side. Earth travels around the sun in one year (365 days). As it travels, different places on Earth are closer to the sun. This is why there are different seasons.

Look at the picture of Earth in December. The North Pole **tilts away from** the sun. This means that the northern hemisphere will be **colder** in December. The South Pole **tilts towards** the sun in December, so that's when the southern hemisphere is **warmer**. This is why it's winter in the northern hemisphere when it's summer in the southern hemisphere.

Find the equator in the diagrams. Why don't countries on the equator have the four seasons? They're at the **centre** of Earth, so they have the **same amount** of sunlight all year.

3 Listen and think. Is it the northern or southern hemisphere?

1
2
3
4

62   Learn about why we have seasons

Culture

4 🎧 2.38 **Listen and read about the different seasons in Argentina. Answer the questions.**

Argentina is a very large country in South America. It's in the southern hemisphere, so winter begins in June and summer begins in December. However, it isn't cold in winter in all of Argentina because it has different climate zones.

Let's look at two examples. The north of Argentina is near the equator and it has a tropical climate. There are lots of rainforests and there are high temperatures all year, even in winter. The south of Argentina has a polar climate. It's close to Antarctica, so it's very cold all year – cold enough for penguins – because it's never near the sun.

In many countries we can say, 'I go skiing in winter and I love swimming in the sea in summer.' You can do those activities in Argentina, but in any season. Why? The Andes is the longest mountain range in the world and 4,000 kilometres of it is on the border between Chile and Argentina. Argentina also has almost 5,000 kilometres of coast from north to south. It's no problem to go skiing in summer and swim in the sea in winter. You only have to choose the correct place!

1 Why are the seasons different in various parts of Argentina?

2 Where are the rainforests?

3 Where is the polar climate zone in Argentina?

4 Can you only find penguins in winter?

5 What's special about the Andes?

6 Are the Andes in Argentina longer than the coast?

5 Make a poster about the seasons in your country. Use your poster to describe the things you like best about each season.

mission STAGE 3

Write some travel advice.

- In your group, think about the weather and prepare travel advice.

  It's snowy in the mountains. You can go skiing! Be careful, there will be ice on the road.

My mission diary
Activity Book page 56

Learn about climate in Argentina

Literature

1 Look at the picture. Name three activities that you can do when it snows. Have you got a favourite snow activity?

🎧 TOMÁS AND THE SNOWMAN
2.39

Tomás and Valentín were brothers. They lived in a small town in Patagonia in Argentina. Tomás was five and Valentín was nine, so they often wanted to do different things.

One day in winter it snowed so much that the hill behind the boys' house became white. Tomás wanted to make a snowman, but Valentín wanted to go snowboarding. 'Will you help your brother make a snowman?' the boys' mum asked. 'Yes,' Valentín said, 'I'll help Tomás make a snowman.'

Tomás and Valentín made a snowman. They called it El Viejo, the old man. It had a scarf around its neck, stones for its eyes and mouth, a carrot for its nose and sticks for its arms. 'I like him,' Tomás said. 'I like him! Let's make a friend for him! I'll get some more sticks and stones from under the trees over there!' Tomás ran to the trees singing, 'Snowman, snowman, lovely, lovely snowman!'

Valentín kicked the snow and said to himself, 'I don't want to make another snowman. I want to go snowboarding.' But what could he do? Then he had an idea. 'I'll knock El Viejo down,' he thought, 'but I'll tell Tomás that the snowman has gone away. Then Tomás will want to go back home and play a different game. And I can go snowboarding!'

Text type: A real-life story

When Tomás came back he was surprised to find that El Viejo wasn't there. 'Where is he?' he said. 'Oh, he walked away down the hill,' Valentín answered. 'I don't know where he was going.' Tomás started crying. 'No!' he said. 'He can't! El Viejo! Come back!' Before Valentín could stop him, Tomás ran back to the house shouting, 'Mummy! Daddy! El Viejo has gone!'

When Valentín got home, he found his brother sitting at the kitchen table. His mother and father looked at him in that special way, the one they used when they weren't pleased with him. Valentín said, 'I'm sorry, Tomás,' and then he asked his brother to go back to the hill. 'We'll make another El Viejo,' he said, 'lots of them.' 'Can we?' Tomás asked. 'Can we, Valentín?' And that was what the brothers did for the rest of the day. They filled the hillside with snowmen. Valentín was happy that his brother was excited and he thought to himself, 'Well, there's always tomorrow – I'll go snowboarding then.'

2 **Role play a conversation with a partner. Imagine you are Tomás and Valentín.**

A You are Tomás. You're very sad about El Viejo. You were very excited when you made him and you were very sad when you saw that El Viejo wasn't there. Tell Valentín how you feel.

> I'm very sad, Valentín. I liked the snowman so much!

B You are Valentín. You're sorry that you made Tomás sad. You only wanted to go snowboarding. Say sorry to Tomás, tell him what happened and talk about the new snowmen you can make together.

> I'm very sorry, Tomás. I didn't want you to be sad. Let's make lots more snowmen. They'll be bigger and better than El Viejo.

Social and emotional skill: Showing remorse

A2 Flyers

1 Talk about the pictures. What are Emma and Robert wearing? What winter sports might they do?

Emma's winter sport

Robert's winter sport

2 Make questions for the answers about Robert's winter sport.

1	Favourite winter sport	His favourite winter sport is skiing.
2	Where	He does it in the mountains.
3	Who / with	He goes with his family.
4	Morning / afternoon	He goes in the afternoon.
5	How long / ski / for	He skis for two hours.

3 Answer the questions about Emma. Choose a word from the box and make a full sentence.

> three   sledging   friends   morning   hills

1 What is Emma's favourite winter sport? _____
2 Where does she go sledging? _____
3 Who does she go sledging with? _____
4 Does she go in the morning or the afternoon? _____
5 How long does she go sledging for? _____

4 In pairs, ask and answer about Emma and Robert. Use the ideas in the box or your own ideas. Invent the answers.

> How old?   What clothes?   Slow / fast?   What time?
> Teacher?   When / lessons?   Has / prize?

How old is Emma?   She's nine.

If you don't understand, say, 'Can you repeat that please?'

Preparation for Speaking Part 2

Review

mission in action!

Act out your TV weather report.

★ Say which country you're covering in your weather report.

This is today's weather report for Canada.

★ Give the weather report in different regions or areas of the country.

It'll be snowy in the mountains.

It's a good time to go skiing in the mountains. Be careful, there'll be ice on the road.

★ Give some travel advice to the audience.

My mission diary
Activity Book page 56

Can you remember?

1. Where's Patagonia?
2. What's the name of the museum that Ivan and the children visited?
3. How will Harry help Mr and Mrs Hill?
4. In which month does summer start in Argentina?
5. What type of climate does the north of Argentina have?
6. What did Valentín want to do in the snow?

Unit consolidation

6 Working together

 1 Watch the video. Ask and answer.

What jobs do you know?
What jobs do robots do?

mission Invent something to help with a job

In this unit I will:

 Choose a job and think what people need for that job.

 Invent and describe something new for the job.

 Make a model of the invention.

 Show the invention at an inventions fair.

Vocabulary 1

1 Listen. Which part is Marc going to play in the new show?

2 🎧 2.41 ▶ Say the chant.

3 Describe a job. Play a guessing game.

— The person who repairs cars.
— I think it's a mechanic.

Jobs

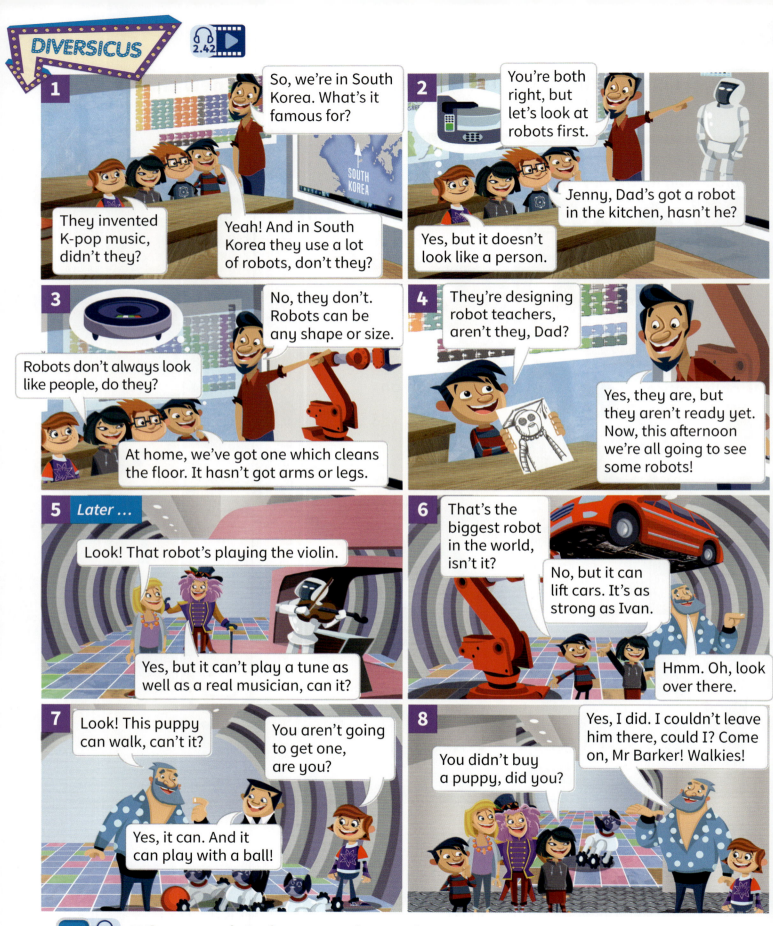

Language practice 1

1 Look at the pictures. What will Barry do in August?

2 Read. Circle the correct tag question.

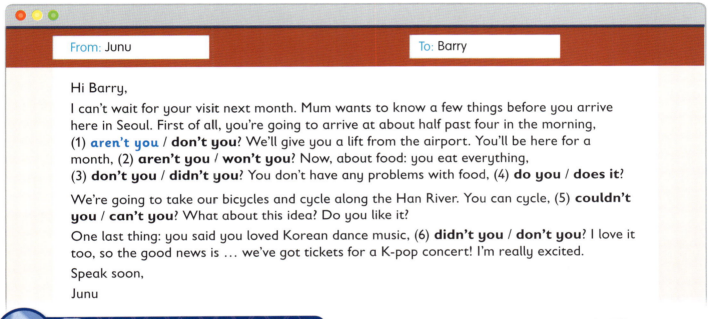

From: Junu To: Barry

Hi Barry,
I can't wait for your visit next month. Mum wants to know a few things before you arrive here in Seoul. First of all, you're going to arrive at about half past four in the morning, (1) **aren't you** / **don't you**? We'll give you a lift from the airport. You'll be here for a month, (2) **aren't you** / **won't you**? Now, about food: you eat everything, (3) **don't you** / **didn't you**? You don't have any problems with food, (4) **do you** / **does it**?

We're going to take our bicycles and cycle along the Han River. You can cycle, (5) **couldn't you** / **can't you**? What about this idea? Do you like it?

One last thing: you said you loved Korean dance music, (6) **didn't you** / **don't you**? I love it too, so the good news is … we've got tickets for a K-pop concert! I'm really excited.
Speak soon,
Junu

🎧 3.03 Grammar spotlight

You eat everything, **don't you**? You can cycle, **can't you**?

3 What do you know about your friend? Write questions. Ask and answer.

> You walk to school by yourself, don't you?
> Yes, I do.

MISSION STAGE 1

Choose a job and think what people need for that job.

- In groups, choose a job and discuss what people need when they do this job.

> Firefighters need to be able to dress quickly. They need a uniform that's easy and quick to put on.

My mission diary
Activity Book page 68

Tag questions 71

Vocabulary 2 and song

1 🎧 3.04 ▶ **Listen and match. Then sing the song.**

1. Firefighters in the **fire station**
   Wearing uniforms on their **fire engine**.
2. Businessmen and businesswomen
   Going to **meetings** in their **offices**.
   World of work! (x4)
3. Police officers by the **police station**
   Wearing uniforms in police cars.
4. Journalists in the street
   Getting **news** for the **newspapers**.
   World of work! (x3)
5. Engineers in **factories**
   With robots making cars.
   World of work! (x4)

2 🎧 3.06 📝 **Listen and write the words.**

3 **Ask and answer about where people work.**

Where do journalists work?

They work in newspaper offices and in the street.

Do you know anyone who works in an office? Who?

72 World of work

Language practice 2

1  **Listen and write.**

Time on Friday morning: 1 _____
Camera shows the man standing near 2 _____
Brother's job: 3 _____
Brother had a meeting with: 4 _____

Grammar spotlight

I didn't go to the bank on Friday morning.	**Didn't you?**
It was my twin brother.	**Was it?**
I was having coffee with the bank manager.	**Were you?**

2 **Choose a situation and write a conversation with a partner. Then act it out.**

- There were some sweets on the table half an hour ago. They aren't there now.
- The tablet was working an hour ago. It isn't working now.
- Your school sweater was on the kitchen chair. Now it's on the floor and it's dirty.

> There were some sweets on the table half an hour ago.

> Were there? I didn't see them …

mission STAGE 2

Think of the job which you've chosen. Invent and describe something that people need to do it.

- In groups, think of ideas for something that can help.
- Choose an idea and draw a sketch of your invention.
- Describe your invention.

> A one-piece suit that is easy and quick to put on for a firefighter.

> It has a helmet, a jacket and boots all in one!

My mission diary
Activity Book page 68

Short questions

Cross-curricular

Inventions and robotics

1 Watch the video.

2 In the past we only used phones to talk to people. Phones have changed a lot. Look at the photos and order them from the earliest phone (1) to the most modern phone (5).

a   b   c   d   e

3 Listen and read. Answer the questions.

An invention begins as an idea. Then other people find ways to make that invention better. Our machines are always changing. Not very long ago, we thought of robots as science fiction, but robots are already part of our lives.

Robots are machines that can do the actions of a human. At first, most robots did boring or dangerous work in factories, like putting parts of cars together or putting chocolate bars in boxes ready to go to the shops. They could repeat the same action all day and never get bored. Those robots didn't need a human to control every action. Other robots need human control. For example, doctors use robots to help them operate on very small body parts. We use robots to test planes and cars. We also have robots which can clean our homes. Some robots drive special cars which don't need a driver and there are even robots on Mars!

Scientists have developed robots that look and behave like humans. They can talk to people, and scientists think they can help in hospitals and schools one day. Do you think it's possible that your future teachers will be robots?

1 What are robots?

2 How can robots make life easier?

3 What do doctors use robots for?

4 What dangerous jobs do robots do

4 Talk to a partner about a robot that you would like to invent.
- How will it help us?
- How will it work?
- What kind of energy does it need?
- Who will want to use this robot?

74 Learn about inventions and robotics

Culture

5 🎧 3.10 **Listen and read. How many of these inventions do you use? Which is the most useful to you? Why?**

South Korea is a country in Asia. It isn't a large country, but more than 50 million people live there. South Korea is one of the most modern and developed countries in the world, with a very important electronics industry.

South Korea also has some of the most interesting ideas in the world of technology. You probably use many of these inventions every day, but did you know that they come from South Korea?

For example, have you got a mobile phone or a tablet? South Korean scientists invented the touch screen. Before this invention, people had to press buttons or use a special kind of pen to give instructions to the machine. It's much easier to give the instructions with your fingers.

South Korea also invented the first MP3 player. In the past, people collected big round records or cassettes of their favourite music. The invention of the MP3 player was the beginning of mobile digital music. You can now take your music with you and listen to it anywhere: on a bus, on a train or in bed. In the past you could take your music with you, but the machines were big and uncomfortable to carry.

Does anyone in your family have a smart card to travel around the city? It's a card that you use to pay for your journeys on buses and trains and it's also a South Korean invention. Have you ever seen an internet café? Again, it's a South Korean invention. You can see why South Korea is so important in the world of technology, can't you?

6 **Find out about other inventors and inventions from your country.**

mission STAGE 3

Make a model of your invention.

- In groups, think of and find materials you can recycle to make your model.

  - We can use old clothes for the model.
  - I've got some old clothes at home which we can use.

- Make a model of your invention.

My mission diary
Activity Book page 68

Learn about South Korean inventions

Literature

1 Would you like to have a robot as a teacher? Why? / Why not?

🎧 3.11 BUDDIE AND SEO-JOON'S ADVENTURE

Scene 1

Narrator: Somewhere in Seoul in the near future …
Buddie is a humanoid robot. He's a teaching assistant in a primary school.
It's his first week at school.

Buddie: Very good! Please repeat.

Kang-dae: He's weird, isn't he! You know like … strange!

Yong-sun: And he isn't human, so he doesn't understand how we feel, does he? He doesn't know how bored we are. He's like a cold fish.

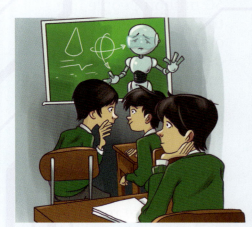

Scene 2

Narrator: One day after class Buddie speaks to Seo-joon.

Buddie: Please help me. No-one in the class likes me. The school is going to send me back to the factory.

Seo-joon: Don't worry, no-one likes me either! They think I'm unfriendly too. Hey! I can teach you about humans!

Buddie: That's a great idea. Thank you! In return, I will help you with your homework.

Seo-joon: Will you? Really? Thanks! I'd love some help with my maths.

Scene 3

Narrator: The following Friday afternoon, Seo-joon gives Buddie some of his clothes and they secretly leave the school together.

Buddie: Mm! I look cool in these!

Seo-joon: Shh! Follow me. We don't want to attract the principal's attention, do we?

Scene 4

Narrator: In the evening, Seo-joon's parents meet Buddie.

Seo-joon: This is Buddie. He's going to help me with maths. He's cool, isn't he?

Parents: Yes, very! How are you?

Buddie: Fine, thank you. I am here to learn about humans … er, help your son.

Seo-joon: Oh no! This is going to be difficult!

Text type: A science-fiction script

Scene 5

Narrator: As the weeks pass, Seo-joon and Buddie become great friends. Seo-joon improves his maths while Buddie learns about humans.

Seo-joon: So, if x=10, the value of $6x-x^2$ is … −40. Yes!

Buddie: This game is wonderful! Come on! I will play you!

Seo-joon: OK, but you'll never win!

Scene 6

Narrator: One Friday night they're leaving school as usual, when suddenly the principal appears.

Principal: Hey! Where are you going?

Seo-joon: Oh no! We're in big trouble now!

Principal: In my office now! Both of you.

Scene 7

Narrator: In the principal's office.

Principal: I'm sending you back to Teacherbot.com immediately.

Seo-joon: I'm sorry. It was my idea. It was wrong, but Buddie has helped me with my maths. I'm getting 'A's now. He's my friend!

Buddie: And Seo-joon has helped me to understand what humans like and do. Now we are friends!

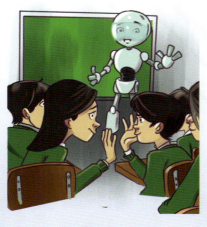

Scene 8

Narrator: A few weeks later in the classroom.

Myung-ok: Wow! I never knew you were so good at maths. Could you help me with my homework this evening? We could play video games after that if you like?

Seo-joon: Sure! Thanks.

Buddie: OK class, today we're going outside to study maths!

Class: Hurray!

Seo-joon: Buddie, you're the best!

2 What problems did Seo-joon and Buddie have? How did they fix them? Do you think they were good friends? Why?

Social and emotional skill: Friendship

A2 Flyers

1 What would you like to know about firefighters? Read the text. Does it answer your questions?

Firefighters

A ___lot___ of cities and villages have firefighters. These are men or women who have **(1)** … how to save people and buildings when there is a fire.

They usually wear a **(2)** … with a helmet, special gloves and strong boots. They always have a torch and **(3)** … they carry a phone **(4)** … they can call their manager for help.

To prepare for **(5)** … job takes 1–4 years. During that time, the men and women practise working in **(6)** … kinds of dangerous places or with different kinds of fires.

There are firefighters at the fire station all day and night. They wait for the sound that tells them to get ready and go to a fire. It takes a good firefighter under a minute to put on a uniform and run to the fire engine. That's fast, **(7)** … it?

One of the firefighters **(8)** … the fire engine. This is not always red and you will find trucks around the world **(9)** … are different colours. It's important to choose a colour which people see **(10)** … at night.

2 Look at the choices for spaces 1–4. Answer the questions.

1	learn	learning	learnt	Which word helps you choose?
2	clothes	uniform	jackets	Which word helps you choose?
3	sometimes	once	never	Why are the other adverbs wrong?
4	while	before	so	Is the text about *why* they carry a phone or *when*?

3 Which choice is correct? Why?

5 these   those   this
6 all   each   every
7 isn't   is   wasn't

8 drives   driving   driven
9 who   where   which
10 easy   easier   easily

Remember, you don't need to think of the words. You choose one of three for each space.

Preparation for Reading and Writing Part 4

Review

mission in action!

6

Show the invention at an inventions fair.

My mission diary
Activity Book page 68

- ⭐ **In groups, describe what the invention is for.**
  - This is an easy-to-wear uniform. You can put it on quickly.

- ⭐ **Describe how you made your invention.**
  - We used recycled clothes.

- ⭐ **Which job is the invention for? Ask the class.**
  - Which job do you think the invention is for?
  - A firefighter!

Can you remember?

1. What's the name of Diversicus's new show? _____
2. What did Ivan buy at the robot exhibition? _____
3. Say two things that Barry's going to do on his trip to Seoul with Junu. _____
4. How can doctors use robots? _____
5. Name three South Korean inventions. _____
6. How did Seo-joon help Buddie? _____

Unit consolidation   79

Review • •• Units 4–6

1 ▶ **Watch the video and do the quiz.**

2 Look at the pictures and answer the questions.

1 What's the weather like?

2 Where are the children in the first picture?

3 What's the girl doing?

4 What's the boy doing?

5 What time is it in the second picture?

6 How are the girl's clothes and the boy's clothes different?

7 What are the girl and the boy doing together?

10:45 a.m.   3:20 p.m.

3 🎧 3.12 **Listen and find the mistakes.**

4 Match the sentence halves. Then add a tag question and ask and answer with a friend.

1 Your dad
2 You were playing
3 Your house
4 She wishes she was
5 Your mum's a
6 Your parents are in
7 School
8 You can snowboard
9 Your favourite
10 You didn't make

a a journalist
b a snowman last winter
c a meeting all day
d pilot
e prepares your lunch
f season is autumn
g starts at 7 a.m.
h is near the station
i very well
j volleyball all day yesterday

> Your dad prepares your lunch, doesn't he?

> No, he doesn't. I prepare it!

Consolidation of units 4–6

5 Read the replies to the teacher's question. Then cover the text and try to remember as many as you can.

School BLOG

Sign out

What will you do which is DIFFERENT this month?

Betty
I'll read the news more.

David
I'll learn to snowboard.

Holly
I'll learn how to repair my own bike.

Frank
I'll prepare lunch for my family! (At least once!)

George
I'll go to the dentist.

Oliver
I'll send more messages to my cousin who's at college in the USA.

Richard
I'll prepare my school uniform before I go to bed each night!

Sarah
I won't be late for school!

Sophia
I won't get angry when my parents ask me to tidy my room!

William
I'll make sure I help my parents more with their business.

6 Ask your classmates for their ideas. Find six things they will change this month. Then write six sentences in your notebook.

I'll start playing tennis.

I'll make sure I do my homework on time.

My friend Jane will start playing tennis.

Consolidation of units 4–6   81

7 Then and now

1 ▶ **Watch the video. Ask and answer.**

Which objects do you use at home every day?
Do you think people in the past had the same objects? Why? / Why not?

mission Create an encyclopedia entry

In this unit I will:

1. Choose a household object.
2. Write a description of it.
3. Talk about how the object has changed over time.
★ Create an encyclopedia entry for it.

Vocabulary 1

1 🎧 3.13 **Listen. What are they going to do in the afternoon?**

Diversicus is in Egypt. Today the Friendly family are on a ship on the River Nile. They're looking at one of their rooms.

gate, oven, telephone, brush, comb, fridge, key, shampoo, soap, shelf, toilet

2 🎧 3.14 ▶ **Say the chant.**

3 🎧 3.15 **Listen and answer the questions.**

Things in the home

Language practice 1

1 Look at the pictures. What do you think George has done during the holidays?

2  Read and circle the correct answer.

Dear Emma,

Can you ¹**see** / **saw** / **seen** the beautiful stamp on the envelope? I'm in Egypt! We've been here for five days and we've ²**found** / **find** / **finding** it really interesting.

We've already ³**driven** / **drove** / **drive** to some of the most important pyramids, but we haven't ⁴**try** / **trying** / **tried** riding camels yet. I ⁵**taken** / **take** / **took** some great photos on our first four days, but my sister ⁶**have** / **hasn't** / **has** just broken my phone. I'm really unhappy about that!

I'm ⁷**wrote** / **writing** / **written** this letter while we're sitting in a café. Dad's ⁸**gone** / **go** / **went** to the car because he and Mum forgot to bring some money, so we can't pay for our drinks until he gets back! I don't mind – it's nice and cool in here.

Love,
George

Grammar spotlight

I've **taken** some great photos.   My sister has just **broken** my phone!

3 Write six questions to ask your classmates. Use these words.

| seen | driven | found | ridden | forgotten |
| broken | stood | fallen | hurt | flown | left | put |

Have you ever stood on a bee?

 **STAGE 1**

Choose a household object.

- In groups, discuss the most useful household objects. Choose one object for your encyclopedia entry.

We can choose a telephone.

Maybe a fridge is better? People have always needed to keep things cold.

Activity Book page 82

Past participles 85

Vocabulary 2 and song

1 🎧 3.19 ▶ **Listen and match. Then sing the song.**

Come on, Jim! Come on, Jenny!
Your room's ¹**untidy**, your room's untidy.
Your room must be tidy when we leave.

We've tidied our room, now our room is ²**tidy**.
We've tidied our room, now our room is tidy.
But my suitcase is ³**full**. It's too ⁴**heavy**.

Now your suitcase is ⁵**broken**, your suitcase is broken.

My suitcase is ⁶**empty** and it's ⁷**light**.
Let's pack this one, put something in mine.
Let's pack this one, put something in mine.
Pack it quickly, it'll be all right.

I've been to town and I've bought this rug.
Isn't it ⁸**unusual**? Isn't it great?
I've been to town and I've bought this rug.
And it wasn't ⁹**expensive**. It was ¹⁰**cheap**.

It isn't a problem. I've got Marc's car.
So put everything in Marc's car.
It's only me! I'm by myself.
It's only me! It'll be all right.

2 🎧 3.21 **Listen and answer the questions.**

3 **In pairs, play the adjective game.**

unhappy   tidy   untidy   broken   heavy   light   empty   full
unusual   expensive   cheap   brave   friendly   popular   unfriendly

Think of something which is heavy.

I think an elephant is heavy. My turn. Think of someone who is brave.

I think my grandpa's brave.

What do you do when something is broken?

Adjectives to describe objects

Language practice 2

1 **Guess which picture they don't talk about in the museum. Listen and check.**

 Grammar spotlight

It **was used for cooking** food.

It **was used to cook** food.

Ovens like this **are used for making** bread and pizza today.

Ovens like this **are used to make** bread and pizza today.

2 **Write definitions for five different things.**

1 It's made of plastic, metal or wood. It's used to sit on and it's got four legs.

3 Play the definitions guessing game.

This is used for looking at your face. It's usually made of glass.

Is it a mirror?

 **STAGE 2**

Describe the household object.

- In groups, write a description of how we use the object.
- Compare different versions of the object.

Fridges are used … to keep food fresh and cold. Some fridges have got an ice machine …

My mission diary

Activity Book page 82

be used for/to

Cross-curricular

Time machines

1 Watch the video.

2 How have objects evolved? Draw a line to match the old and modern objects in the photos.

3 Listen and read. Match the words in blue with the photos (1–6).

We use machines to help us in different ways: to work, travel, communicate … or to have fun. There are simple machines, with only one or no moving parts, like a screw ⟨⟩, and complex machines, with many parts that work together, like a clock.

'Time to get up!' Clocks control modern life. Today, we nearly always know the time, but early humans didn't worry about it. They hunted and worked when it was light and they slept at night. However, as civilisations developed, humans wanted to know the time.

The Egyptians built enormous towers and used shadows and the sun to tell the time. Later, people used a smaller version of this, called a sundial ☐, but this can't help on cloudy days or at night. For hundreds of years people marked and burnt candles or they used a water clock ☐ or an hourglass ☐, which used sand.

The 14th century mechanical clock ☐ was a European invention. It rang a bell every hour. Clockmakers added the hour and minute hands. A clock with hands is called an analogue clock ☐ and a digital clock ☐ only has numbers. Our clocks today are much more accurate than earlier versions and they're everywhere: on our computers, tablets, phones and even in the street. No-one should be late these days!

88 Learn about the evolution of objects

Culture

4 🎧 3.25 **Listen and read. Answer the questions.**

The Ancient Egyptians were one of the earliest human civilisations to develop and their inventions were amazing. 3,000 years ago, their technology helped them build the pyramids and royal palaces. They had their own writing called hieroglyphics and they made paper from the papyrus plant.

The pyramids in Egypt are some of the most impressive things that humans have built. When a pharaoh (their king) died, the people buried him inside a pyramid. There are about 140 pyramids. The largest is the Pyramid of Khufu or the Great Pyramid of Giza, which was about 150 metres tall. We can see that they used enormous blocks of rock, but there are some important questions. How did the Ancient Egyptians bring the rocks to the place where they were building the pyramid? How did they lift the rocks to the top?

Experts think that they brought the rocks down the River Nile on rafts. They didn't have the machines that we have today, but they had simple machines like ramps and levers. The workers cut the rocks and moved them slowly up the pyramid on ramps which they built around the sides. They lifted the heavy rocks with levers and built the pyramids one rock at a time. Archaeologists think it took 23 years, and thousands of people, to complete the Great Pyramid of Giza.

1 Why did the Ancient Egyptians build the pyramids?

2 How did the River Nile help the pyramid builders?

3 Which simple machines did the Ancient Egyptians use to build the pyramids?

4 How long did it take to build the Great Pyramid of Giza?

Fun fact!

Did you know that the Ancient Egyptians also invented toothpaste? They had problems with their teeth because their bread had a lot of sand in it.

mission STAGE 3

Research the history and evolution of your household object.
- Find out about earlier versions of your item.
- Use the internet and encyclopedias to help you make notes.

Egyptians used jars full of water to keep food cold.

My mission diary

Activity Book page 82

Learn about the pyramids of Ancient Egypt

Literature

1 What do you know about Ancient Egypt? Look at the picture and find three mistakes.

🎧 3.26 THE BOY KING

In 1922, an archaeologist found the tomb of an Ancient Egyptian king, a pharaoh, called Tutankhamun, who we sometimes call King Tut. Tutankhamun died when he was 19. An x-ray showed he had a broken leg, but we don't know much about his life. People have different ideas about what happened to him, but no-one knows for sure. Here's a story about what may have happened to him.

Once upon a time in a city called Akhetaten in Ancient Egypt, there was a boy called Tut. Tut was a happy child, but when he was only nine years old his father died. The great men of the royal court told him that he was now the country's new king, which they called 'pharaoh'. That was the end of Tut's happy days as a child.

Tut didn't know how to be a king, but no-one let him decide what to do anyway. The real rulers of the land were a general named Horemheb and a man called Ay. They wanted to control Tut and they wanted him to do everything they said. Tut hated them both.

Text type: A historical fiction story

A year later Horemheb and Ay told Tut to marry a beautiful young girl. Her name was Ank. Tut had everything that a pharaoh needed, but he was bored!

When Tut was 18, Horemheb and Ay gave him a new pair of sandals. They were expensive, but there was nothing special about them. Or was there? There were faces on the bottom of the sandals.

'That's unusual,' Tut thought. He asked 'Why are these faces here?'
'They are the faces of your enemies,' Horemheb explained. 'These sandals are used for standing on them.' Tut was very interested and he put on the sandals.

As soon as Tut was alone, he took them off again. Who were his real enemies? Horemheb and Ay, of course. They were horrible and they never let him do what he wanted. Tut carefully painted Horemheb's and Ay's faces onto the bottom of his new sandals. Then he put them on, he went outside and he jumped up and down in the hot sand!

Later that day, Horemheb and Ay gave Tut a board game. Tut and Ank started to play. Horemheb and Ay stood behind them, watching the game. Suddenly a piece fell off the board. Tut jumped up to get it, but something made him fall over. Did he fall or was he pushed? No-one will ever know, but his leg was broken. It was a very bad break. Tut became sick and died. Ay married Ank and became the next pharaoh.

2 **Everyone in Egypt thought Horemheb and Ay worked very hard to help Tut to be king, but Tut didn't like them. Do you think Tut was right or wrong? Give reasons.**

Social and emotional skill: Taking a different perspective

A2 Flyers

1 Look at this story title and the picture. What can you see? What is the woman doing?

> Mrs Stamp's new phone

2 Read the sentences on the left.

Examples Mrs Stamp lives in America and works for the police. She decided to buy a new phone for all the messages when she's at work.	Mrs Stamp is an **police** / **American police** officer. She gets a lot of messages so she **needed** / **used** a new phone.
1 Her car wasn't working, so her husband David drove her to a shop near his office.	She and her husband went **by car** / **for a walk** to a shop near where he works.
2 Mrs Stamp suddenly saw a black and silver one, which she liked.	Mrs Stamp preferred the phone which **had two colours** / **suddenly rang**.
3 She paid for it and David took her home.	David drove his wife home **after** / **before** she bought the phone.
4 At half past six, Mrs Stamp walked into the kitchen to make their dinner and feed their cat, Holly.	At half past six, she went **to prepare** / **to eat** everyone's dinner.
5 The cat was sitting on the floor and the phone was next to her, in pieces.	Holly was **next to** / **sitting on** the broken phone.
6 Mrs Stamp started to shout, so David went to see why.	David **could hear his wife** / **couldn't see Holly** because she was making a loud noise.
7 'I love our cat, but she's very naughty! Look at my phone!'	**Mrs Stamp** / **David** says that Holly is very naughty.

Who is Holly? Why is she naughty?

3 Look at the sentences on the right. They must have the same meaning as the sentences on the left. Choose the right word(s).

> Be careful! The picture doesn't give you any answers. All the words you need for your answers are in the story.

Preparation for Reading and Writing Part 5

Review

mission in action!

Create an encyclopedia entry.

★ Write a short description of the object. Include information about the history of the object.

Fridges are used to keep food in good condition and to keep food cold. Egyptians used jars full of water to keep food cold. Later, people …

★ Draw pictures or add photographs of the object.

★ Share your encyclopedia entry with the class.

We chose a fridge. People have always needed to keep things cold. The history in our entry starts thousands of years ago with the Ancient Egyptians.

My mission diary
Activity Book page 82

Can you remember?

1 Which river did the Friendly family sail on? _____
2 Who fell off a camel in Egypt? _____
3 What hasn't George done on his holiday yet? _____
4 What type of clock uses the sun? _____
5 What was the problem with Ancient Egyptian bread? _____
6 Why did King Tut dislike Horemheb and Ay? _____

Unit consolidation

8 Space travel

 Watch the video. Ask and answer.

What can you see in the sky during the day / at night?
What do you know about space?

mission — Plan a space mission

In this unit I will:

 Decide with my group where we're going and what we will do and see there.

 Give instructions on how to fly the spaceship.

3. Decide what to take on our mission.

Give a report to journalists on Earth.

Vocabulary 1

1 🎧 3.27 Listen. What's Pablo going to write?

Diversicus is in Italy. This morning the children and Ivan are learning about deep space at the Galileo Museum.

17th CENTURY SPACE

moon · engine · spaceship · star · rocket · space · astronaut · telescope · planet

2 🎧 3.28 ▶ Say the chant.

3 🎧 3.29 Listen and say *yes* or *no*.

In space | 95

Language practice 1

1 Look at the pictures. What do you think the astronaut is going to do on holiday?

2 Read and complete the dialogue with A–E.

Journalist: Hello, Betty. You've just come back from space, haven't you?
Betty Queen: ¹ __C__
Journalist: Do you think people will have holidays on the moon in the future?
Betty Queen: ² ____
Journalist: And will space travellers have to wear enormous spacesuits?
Betty Queen: ³ ____
Journalist: So, what are your plans for the next few weeks? You're going to be on holiday, aren't you?
Betty Queen: ⁴ ____
Journalist: Ooh, are you going to watch space films?
Betty Queen: ⁵ ____

A No, we aren't. We're going to watch films about adventures at home!
B Yes, I do. Spaceships will improve and they'll carry more people.
C Yes, that's right. I arrived at the Space Centre two days ago.
D Yes, I am, and I'm going to watch films with my children.
E I don't think so. They'll be smaller and helmets won't be as heavy as now.

🎧 3.32 Grammar spotlight

Spaceships **will** improve.   **Are** you **going to** watch space films?

3 What do you think will change in the future?

> I think children won't go to school.

4 What are you going to do this weekend? Ask and answer.

 **STAGE 1**

Decide on a space mission.
- In groups, decide what you're going to do.
- Discuss what you think you'll see.

> We're going to go to Mars and we're going to look for life there. I think we'll see some aliens.

My mission diary
Activity Book page 94

will and *going to*

Vocabulary 2 and song

1 🎧 3.33 ▶ **Listen and match. Then sing the song.**

Can you ¹**touch** the stars?
²**Follow** the Milky Way!
Can you explore space today?

Go into your rocket, through the ³**entrance**.
⁴**Turn on** your engine. See Earth disappear.
See the moon appear. ⁵**Land** on the red planet.
⁶**Turn off** your engine, put on your spacesuit.

Put on your helmet. Pick up your flag.
Leave your spaceship, through the ⁷**exit**.
Put your flag into the ground.
Take pictures for the news and the internet.

⁸**Enter** your spaceship. Prepare your dinner.
⁹**Save** some moon cheese for me.
Save some moon cheese for me.
Come back to Earth.
Sit in the armchair, watch films on TV.
¹⁰**Stay** at home. Stay at home.

2 **Imagine you work for a Space Mission. Write instructions for an astronaut to go into deep space. Use the words in the box.**

> enter   land   stay   touch   turn on   turn off   follow

1   Enter the spaceship.

3 **Read your instructions for a friend to act out.**

> Would you like to go to space? Why? / Why not?

Adventure words

Language practice 2

1 🎧 3.35 **Listen and order the pictures.**

a  b  c

 🎧 3.36 **Grammar spotlight**

Ivan **landed** his rocket on the new planet.

Something **was moving** behind the door!

He **was turning off** his engine **when** he **heard** a strange noise.

2 📝 **Finish the sentences to write a different story. Tell it to a friend.**

3 📝 **Write about things which happened last week.**

I was … when …
My (sister) was … when …
We were … when …

Ivan was turning on the engine when …
He was putting on his helmet when …
He was leaving the spaceship when …
Ivan was flying through space when …

 **STAGE 2**

Give spaceship instructions.

- In groups, give instructions to fly the spaceship. Include a diagram.

Press the green button to turn on the engine.

Please don't touch the yellow button!

Enter your secret number.

My mission diary
Activity Book page 94

Review of past tenses

Cross-curricular

Preparing for Mars

1 Watch the video.

2 Match the words to the photos.

> 1 moon landing 2 spacewalk 3 Mars 4 rusty iron

3 🎧 3.37 Listen and read. Answer the questions.

Mars is the fourth planet from the sun. It's called 'the red planet' because iron oxide (rusty iron) gives the surface this colour. Mars is a cold, desert world and, like Earth, it has seasons and weather. Scientists want to know if Mars had living things in the past. They think that in the past there was liquid water on the planet.

NASA believes that it will be possible to send astronauts to Mars by 2030. We have to know what dangers there are and find a way to protect the astronauts. This is why there have been robots on Mars for many years.

The robots send information back to Earth about the rocks and atmosphere on Mars and scientists design materials to help astronauts to survive there.

How can we prepare people on Earth for a Mars mission? Different groups of six scientists have spent eight months in a special dome. Could people live in a small group out of contact with their friends and families, with no phones or messages? Yes! The experiments have worked and the mission plans continue.

1 Why have we sent robots to Mars?

2 What do these robots do?

3 Would you like to go to Mars? Why? / Why not?

4 Look at the table. Compare Earth and Mars.

	Size (diameter)	Days in a year	Hours in a day	Moons	Name and surface information
Earth	12,742 km	365	24	1	'the blue planet' (water)
Mars	6,779 km	687	25	2	'the red planet' (iron oxide)

Learn about space exploration

Culture

5 🎧 3.38 **Listen and read. Answer the questions.**

HOME | STORIES | PHOTOS

The International Space Station (the ISS) is a huge science laboratory in space where astronauts can live and work. The astronauts come from different countries, but they must be able to speak English and Russian. It's quite difficult living on a space station because there is no gravity. Everything floats, so there are special ways to have a shower, wash your hair and go to the toilet on a space station.

On Earth, we're always moving against gravity (except when we're asleep) and this helps us to keep fit. If astronauts don't exercise, they become weak and they have serious health problems when they return to Earth. This is why the astronauts have a very strict exercise programme, but they can't play sports like basketball. Can you think why?

Life is difficult in space, but Italian astronaut Samantha Cristoforetti brought her coffee machine! How could you make **your** stay on the ISS more like home?

1 Why do you think the astronauts must speak English and Russian?

2 What activities are difficult for astronauts because there is no gravity?

6 🎧 3.39 **Read again and complete the fact file. Listen and add the missing information.**

 STAGE 3

Decide what to take on your mission and say why.

> We're going to take cameras to take photos.

> We're going to take extra spacesuits because …

My mission diary
Activity Book page 94

FACT FILE
- Name: Cristoforetti
- Date of birth:
- Nationality:
- First job:
- Profession now:
- Days at the ISS:

Learn about an Italian astronaut at the ISS **101**

Literature

1 Do the space quiz with a partner.

1 How many planets are there in our solar system? Circle the correct answer.
   A Six.   B Seven.   C Eight.

2 Which planet is called 'the red planet'?
   A Mars.   B Earth.   C Venus.

3 What do you call a science laboratory in space?
   A A space mission.   B A space station.   C A space office.

THE SPACE BLOG

BLOG POST 1: DAY ONE

Hello! This is Elena Romano. I'm on board Explorer One with Luca Rossi. Luca and I were the very lucky winners of a competition to become the first children to go into space. We're travelling with two astronauts called Leo and Melita and I'm going to write about what happens. This will be an exciting adventure!

BLOG POST 2: DAY THREE

I've had some questions from people on Earth. Everyone asked, 'Are you afraid?' No, we aren't. We feel very safe up here! Sally from Canada asked, 'What's the best thing about space?' That's easy – looking out of the window at planet Earth. It's so beautiful! Luca's favourite thing is zero gravity. Every few minutes he says, 'Come on, let's fly!'

BLOG POST 3: DAY FIVE

Nikos in Athens wants to know the worst thing about space. The food, Nikos! There is no word to describe it. It's just – eurrrghhhh! Luca says he wants to eat a bowl of his grandmother's pasta. Me too, Luca, me too!

Text type: A science-fiction story

BLOG POST 4: DAY SEVEN

Something in the rocket is making a strange noise. Melita says everything is OK, but I saw her talking to Leo earlier. They both looked worried.

BLOG POST 5: DAY EIGHT (morning)

This morning Luca and I were looking out of the window when Leo appeared. 'Bad news,' he said. 'The engine isn't working very well.' Luca asked, 'What's going to happen?' Leo didn't answer for a long, long time. Finally, he said, 'I don't know.'

BLOG POST 6: DAY EIGHT (afternoon)

This is getting frightening. The lights on the spaceship are turning on and off. Leo and Melita are going from place to place, fetching things to try to fix the engine. They've told us not to worry, but we don't know what's going to happen. Luca thinks we'll be lost in space forever. Will we ever get home?

BLOG POST 7: DAY EIGHT (evening)

We're nearly home! Leo and Melita asked us to fly the spaceship for them while they fixed the engine. Well, the spaceship's computer flies the spaceship, but we had to watch the screen and make sure that the blue light was on and that we were moving from left to right on the screen! 'You've been brilliant!' Melita said. 'We've fixed the engine. You two can have a rest now while Leo and I take us home. Why don't you have some space food while we slowly go back to Earth?'

2 Work with a partner. Role play a conversation.

A You are Luca. You're very worried about the spaceship's engine. You think you might not get back to Earth. Tell Elena how you feel.

B You are Elena. You're also worried about the spaceship's engine, but you think the astronauts can fix it. Tell Luca how you feel.

> I'm worried about the engine. Do you think we'll get back to Earth?

> Well, it's a strange noise, but Leo and Melita are very clever. I'm sure …

3 What do you do when you feel worried or frightened?

Social and emotional skill: Managing own emotions

A2 Flyers

1 **Read these sentences from a story about a trip to a cinema. Where didn't people want to live in the film?**

1 Yesterday, William and his cousin Katy watched a film about a red planet at the cinema.

(1 adjective and 1 verb in the past)

2 'I really want to be an astronaut.'

(1 present simple and 1 singular noun)

3 'I think it'll be frightening because space is enormous. I don't really like adventures!'

(1 plural noun and 1 future verb)

4 At the end of the film people were living in strange, new cities on the red planet because no-one wanted to live on Earth.

(3 adjectives)

2 **Find examples of the words in brackets ( ) for each sentence.**

3 **Read the end of the story. What's missing: an adjective, a noun or a verb?**

'That was **(1)** _____,' said Katy's dad, 'but I like living on our **(2)** _____ , I hope we can stay here!'
'Me too!' **(3)** _____ William. 'Will children go to school on that planet?'
'Perhaps there'll be schools for aliens and people in the future!' said Katy's dad. 'But now let's go and have some **(4)** _____.'
'That's a great **(5)** _____,' said William and everyone agreed.

> Remember to read all of the story once before you start completing the spaces. This will help you understand what the story is about.

4 **Choose the best word for each space.**

☐ interesting ☐ ice cream ☐ said ☐ idea ☐ cinema
☐ interested ☐ homework ☐ spoke ☐ planet

104 Preparation for Reading and Writing Part 3

Review

mission in action!

Give a report to journalists on Earth.

★ You're talking to journalists. Present your team.

This is the Rocket team …

★ Explain what and where your mission was.

We went to look for life on Mars …

★ Say what you found.

We took lots of photos of Mars, but we didn't find life there!

My mission diary
Activity Book page 94

Can you remember?

1 Which museum did Ivan and the children visit?
2 What's Pablo's astronaut going to travel in?
3 Where has Betty Queen just travelled back from?
4 What do some people call Mars?
5 What unusual thing did Samantha Cristoforetti take into space?
6 Why were Elena and Luca frightened on day eight of their journey?

9 Great bakers

1 Watch the video. Ask and answer.

What did you have for lunch yesterday?
Do you like cooking? Who do you cook with?

mission Take part in a cooking competition

In this unit I will:

 Create a cooking challenge.

 Discuss the ingredients in your creation.

 Complete a cooking challenge.

★ Present your creation and vote for the best.

Vocabulary 1

1 🎧 4.02 **Listen. What does Grandpa have to cut for Jenny?**

Today Diversicus is in Cambridge, England. The children are helping Grandma and Grandpa Friendly to prepare lunch.

- snacks
- piece (of pizza)
- pizza
- knife
- fork
- salt
- pepper
- spoon
- olives

2 🎧 4.03 ▶ **Say the chant.**

3 🎧 4.04 **Who says it? Listen and say the name.**

Mealtimes and snacks

Language practice 1

1 **Circle the words to complete the text.**

School Bake Off   by Harry Green

Last week there was a school cake competition. At the end, the teacher tried to use a microphone to say the winners' names, but it made a loud noise. It ¹**tasted** / **sounded** like someone playing an electric guitar very badly!

The cake which won first prize ²**smelt** / **looked** like a big bird's nest with gold eggs in it. I touched the nest and it ³**tasted** / **felt** like dry grass, but it was cereal! It ⁴**sounded** / **smelt** like carrot cake, but I wanted to know what it ⁵**looked** / **tasted** like.

In the end, the winner gave me a piece … and yes, it was carrot cake and it tasted ⁶**delicious** / **noisy**.

🎧 4.07 Grammar spotlight

I wanted to know what it **tasted like**.   It **felt like** dry grass.

It **smelt like** carrot cake.   It **looked like** a nest.

It **sounded like** someone playing an electric guitar.

2 🎧 4.08 **Listen. What does it sound like?**

3 **What does it look like?**

①    ②    ③

mission STAGE 1

Create a cooking challenge.

- In groups, think of a cooking challenge and create a challenge card.

  > You have to create a delicious snack that doesn't use salt …

- Give your cooking challenge card to another group.

My mission diary

Activity Book page 106

It smells/tastes/looks/feels/sounds like …

Vocabulary 2 and song

1 🎧 4.09 ▶ **Listen and match. Then sing the song.**

We're having a surprise party
For the end of the tour.
We're making afternoon tea.
Let's bake some more!

¹**Biscuits** are made of this:
²**Butter**, ³**honey**, ⁴**flour** and ⁵**eggs**.
I've turned on the ⁶**cooker**,
So the ⁷**oven**'s hot.
I've ⁸**baked** the biscuits.
We've got a lot.

Chorus

Mix the cake in the bowl:
⁹**Sugar** and butter, eggs and flour.
Put it in the oven.
Let it bake for an hour.
Put some ¹⁰**jam** in the middle,
Then go and ¹¹**wash up** …. Wash up!

Chorus (x2)

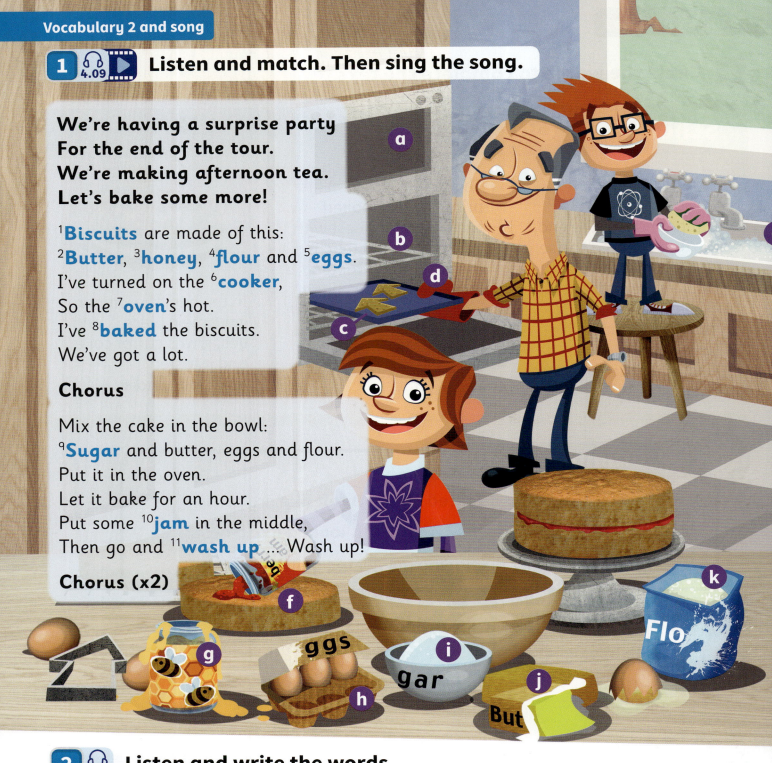

2 🎧 4.11 **Listen and write the words.**

3 📝 **Imagine you've just baked a special cake. Draw and write about it.**

- What ingredients did you mix together?
- How long was it in the oven?
- Who's it for?
- What does it look, taste and smell like?

Do you like to cook? What's your favourite recipe?

110 Cooking

Language practice 2

9

1 Listen. What will Betty help Frank to do before they go to the park?

> **Grammar spotlight**
>
> The smell's **making me hungry**.
> It **made me** really **happy**.
> It **made us hot** and **thirsty**.

2 Write two answers for each question.

1 What makes you happy?   *My kitten makes me happy.*

2 What makes you angry?

3 What makes you sad?

4 What makes you worried?

5 What makes you frightened?

3 Ask and answer with a friend. Are any of your answers the same?

mission STAGE 2

Complete the cooking challenge.
- In your group, read the challenge and decide what you're going to cook.
- List the ingredients. Think about how you'll present your creation.

> I think we can bake a cake with eggs, flour and butter.

> But will people need a fork? The challenge said 'eat it without a fork'.

> I know! We can cut it into small pieces.

My mission diary
Activity Book page 106

make somebody + adjective — 111

Cross-curricular

How chocolate is made

1 ▶ Watch the video.

2 What do you eat that comes from both plants and animals?

_____

3 🎧 4.14 Listen and read. Then find the missing words and write the sentences in the correct order.

 The cacao tree grows in hot climate zones. It has small white flowers and some of these flowers grow fruit called pods. The pods can be as big as footballs. When the pods are ready, they change colour and workers cut them down from the tree.

They open the pods and take out the beans. Inside the pods, there are 20 to 50 beans. The beans dry in the sun. The workers then put the beans into sacks and send them to the factory.

Next, they crush the beans and take out the cocoa liquid. This isn't sweet – it's very bitter.

At the factory, they clean and cook the beans.

They have to add sugar and sometimes milk to the cocoa liquid to make it sweet.

Finally, they heat the mixture so they can make different shapes with it. What does your favourite chocolate bar look like?

a   Then they mix the cocoa liquid with _____ and milk.
b   People cut down the pods when they are ready and take out the _____
c   They send the beans to the _____, where people clean and cook them.
d   They heat the mixture and make it into different _____.
e   The beans dry in the _____.

112 Learn about chocolate production

Culture

4 🎧 4.15 **Listen and read about a popular meal in the UK. Where's it from?**

Traditional foods use ingredients that people can find locally – that's why they are traditional. For example, China grows rice, so rice usually accompanies a Chinese meal. Fish and chips developed as a traditional meal on the UK coast because it was easy to buy fish (and potatoes, of course).

These days, one of the most popular meals in the UK is not British. Do you recognise the food in the photo? This is curry, with rice, Indian bread and the other things that usually accompany it. The curries that people eat in the UK are originally from India, Pakistan and Bangladesh. Curry has become an important part of British life and 23 million people in the UK say that they eat curry regularly. Some people like very hot, spicy curries, but others prefer a milder curry. Have you ever tried curry? And would you like yours spicy?

5 🎧 4.16 **Listen and match the traditional UK food to the photos.**

1 fish and chips   2 shepherd's pie   3 Victoria sponge cake   4 roast beef   5 trifle

a    b    c    d    e

6 Talk about your favourite traditional meal.

> My favourite meal is … . It's got … . It's made with … and it's delicious!

mission STAGE 3

Discuss the ingredients in your creation.

- Think about where you found the ingredients for your creation and whether they came from animals or plants.

> We used honey from the bees in our village.

My mission diary

Activity Book page 106

Learn about traditional food in the UK   113

Literature

1 Look at the pictures. What kind of adventures do you think the gingerbread girl has?

🎧 4.17

THE GINGERBREAD GIRL'S ADVENTURE

Every Saturday morning Bruno gets up at 5 a.m. to make gingerbread people. He carefully measures the ingredients and puts them into a large mixing bowl, with a big smile. As he bakes, he listens to his favourite music and sings along happily. Later, he and his dad take the warm, freshly baked gingerbread people to Spring Wood, a local home for older people.
The gingerbread people taste so delicious that everyone in London knows about them.

One Saturday morning, the doorbell rang. Bruno opened the door and a man walked in. The man took a deep breath.

'Ah gingerbread!' he said. 'It smells just like my old granny's kitchen, and I'm sure it tastes delicious, too. Sorry, I'm Mr Brett,' he added. 'I have cake shops all over London and I'd like you to bake your special gingerbread for me. You could become very rich!'

'Really?' Bruno said, surprised. 'But I just use a traditional recipe.'

'No secret, extra, special ingredient …?' Mr Brett asked.

'No. Let me get Dad – you can ask him too,' Bruno replied.

When Bruno went upstairs, Mr Brett saw a basket of gingerbread people on the hall table. He took one, a gingerbread girl, put it into his pocket and left very quickly.

The gingerbread girl was afraid. When Mr Brett stopped moving, she looked around. She was in a huge bakery.

'I have a new biscuit! Crush it up and find out what the secret ingredient is!' she heard Mr Brett say.

114 Text type: A fairy tale adaptation

Oh no! The gingerbread girl didn't like that idea – and Bruno and the people at Spring Wood needed her. She had to do something fast!

At that moment, Mrs Brett came in. 'I'm going to the market to get some ingredients now.'

When the gingerbread girl heard that, she quickly jumped into Mrs Brett's handbag.

Mrs Brett left the bakery and caught a bus. The gingerbread girl looked out of the window at all the famous sights of London: Big Ben, the London Eye, … and she saw crowds of people.

Then something amazing happened. She saw Bruno and his dad in the street. The next time the bus stopped, she jumped off and a big black taxi almost crushed her. Finally, she caught up with Bruno and jumped into his coat pocket.

As soon as Bruno and his dad arrived at Spring Wood, they gave out the gingerbread people. When Bruno came to the last lady, there weren't any left. He couldn't understand it. He always made 50! Checking the basket again, he saw a gingerbread girl lying in the bottom.

'Oh, here she is,' he said. He didn't know anything about the gingerbread girl's great adventure.

As he gave the old lady her gingerbread, she smiled and said, 'These biscuits make me so happy. They taste like a bit of home every Saturday! You must put a lot of love into them.'

Bruno smiled and said, 'Yes, that's my secret, extra, special ingredient – love.'

2 **The old lady knows that Bruno makes his biscuits with love. Tell a partner about something that someone does, or has done, for you which felt like this.**

> My grandma always makes birthday biscuits with my name on them.

Social and emotional skill: Being passionate about what you do

A2 Flyers

1 Match the verbs in box A with the words in box B. How many different phrases can you make?

A
- take
- give
- make
- be
- visit
- taste
- leave

B
- someone a piece of cake
- delicious
- a photo
- a market
- a cake
- something in the oven
- on a tour

2 Make sentences using the phrases.

> Last year, I visited a really cool market in Vienna.

> My brother left a pizza in the oven yesterday and it smelt horrible!

3 Harry is writing a holiday diary. Find two mistakes.

> I is on a cooking tour with my uncle. This morning we went into town and we visit a market. In the afternoon, we learnt to prepare pasta with a meat sauce. It wasn't very difficult. (I often make something like that at home.)

4 Read the rest of his diary. Write a word for each space. Look at the phrases in Activity 1 to help you, but you need to change some of the words.

> Then we **(1)** _a coconut cake_ . It only needed to cook for 25 minutes, but I left mine **(2)** _____ the oven too long, so it burnt! It didn't matter. The cook gave us each a **(3)** _____ of her cake. It tasted **(4)** _____ , of course, and it looked great too, so I **(5)** _____ a photo!
>
> Tomorrow's lesson is a snack with olives and tomatoes. No problem!

When you finish, it's a good idea to re-read all the text and check spelling and meaning.

Preparation for Reading and Writing Part 6

Review

mission in action!

Vote for the best creation.

★ In your groups, read your challenge card aloud.

Our cooking challenge was to create a delicious snack that you can eat without a fork.

★ Describe and show your creation.

We made a cake that you can eat without a fork. We made it with …

★ As a class, vote for the best creation.

My mission diary
Activity Book page 106

Can you remember?

1. Who do the children prepare lunch with in Cambridge?
2. What does Grandpa Friendly think looks like spaghetti?
3. What did the cake that won the School Bake Off look like?
4. What type of climate do cacao trees grow in?
5. Name three traditional UK dishes.
6. Why did Mr Brett take the gingerbread girl?

Unit consolidation

Review • • • Units 7–9

1 ▶ Watch the video and do the quiz.

2 🎧 4.18 Listen and say the word. Write the word under each picture.

> A knife – that's picture e!

a.
b.
c.
d.
e.
f.
g.
h.

3 Practise with a friend.   *What's this used for?*   *It's used for …*

4 Complete the chart. Think of questions to ask your friends. Use *What makes you … ?* Write their answers in the chart.

| happy | unhappy | hungry | tired | angry | bored | frightened | thirsty |

Name	Question	Answer
Helen	What makes you happy?	Listening to rock music.

> Helen, what makes you happy?   *Listening to rock music makes me happy.*

118 Consolidation of units 7–9

5 **Read the email. What two snacks does Helen write about?**

From: Helen　　　　　　　　　　　To: Oliver

Hi Oliver,

How are you? I want to tell you about my trip to the city space museum two days ago. I've never been before so I was very excited! I was looking after my little sister and she was bored so I said 'We're going on an adventure!' Adventures make her happy! ☺

When we arrived, we started to explore. It's enormous, not expensive and full of interesting and exciting objects to touch.

The first room you enter looks like deep space. There is information about different planets with a quiz at the end. The winner can invent a name for a planet – that's exciting, isn't it? The next room looks like the inside of a spaceship. You can touch an astronaut's spacesuit (I don't know how an astronaut can wear it – it looks really heavy!) and you can see where the astronauts prepare their food – did you know they use a knife, fork and spoon to eat? I didn't – I thought it was all in bags.

We were looking at the oven from the spaceship when my sister said she was hungry, so we went to have a snack. They were preparing a pizza in the restaurant and the smell of food always makes me hungry so we had a piece of pizza with olives! It was delicious. While we were eating the pizza, they were baking biscuits, so we bought some. Don't worry! We have left some for you – you will love them! They look like rockets and taste like honey!

After lunch, we explored more of the museum and stayed for the rest of the day. They were turning off the lights when we left!

Have you ever been to a museum?

See you soon,

Helen

6 **Read the email again and complete the sentences.**

1 Helen and her sister went to a _____ .
2 The museum is _____ and not _____ .
3 Helen thought the _____ looked heavy.
4 Helen didn't know astronauts _____ .
5 Helen and her sister ate _____ .
6 They have left _____ for Oliver. They look like _____ and _____ .

7 **Imagine you're Oliver. Write a postcard to Helen and tell her about your trip to a museum. Use these questions to help you.**

Where did you go?　Who did you go with?　When did you go?　What did you see?
What did you have to eat?　What was the most exciting thing you saw?

Grammar reference

Unit 1

might/may

We use *might* and *may* to talk about things we aren't sure about in the present or the future.

| I / You / He/She / We / They | might / may | (not) | **go** to the ski centre. |

I might not enjoy skiing.

Indefinite pronouns

- We use indefinite pronouns to talk about a place, person or thing without saying which one.
- We use pronouns with *every-* to talk about **all** of something.
  Luca ate **everything** on his plate, and then asked for more.
- We use pronouns with *some-* to talk about **one** of something.
  We should eat **something** before we go out.
- We use pronouns with *any-* for **asking questions.**
  Are you hungry? Would you like **anything** to eat?
- We use pronouns with *no-* to talk about **none** of something.
  There's **nothing** to eat at home. Shall we go to a restaurant for lunch?

We use *-where* to talk about places, *-one* to talk about people and *-thing* to talk about things.

	all	+	-/?	-
	every	some	any	no
where	everywhere	somewhere	anywhere	nowhere
thing	everything	something	anything	nothing
one	everyone	someone	anyone	no-one

Everyone should come to the circus!

120 Grammar reference

Past tense review: regular and irregular verbs; past simple with *ago*

- To make the past simple tense, we usually add *-ed* to the end of the base form of the verb.
- There are lots of irregular verbs in the past tense. You can check the past tense of some important verbs on p127.

    When we **got** home, we **sat** down and we **told** my mum all about our trip.
- To make a negative, we use *did* + *not* + verb in base form.
- To make a question, we use (question word +) *did* + pronoun (e.g. *she*, *you*) + base form of the verb.

I		I		
You		You		
He/She/It	**stayed** on the beach. **broke** the tent.	He/She/It	**didn't**	**stay** on the beach. **break** the tent.
We		We		
They		They		

What	did	I	say?	
	Did	you he/she/it we they	say	something?

We saw lots of amazing animals.

- We use *ago* to say when something in the past happened.

    Pablo arrived three days **ago**.

Remember:
did not = didn't

too and *enough*

- We use *too* (*much/many*) when we want less of something. We use (*not*) *enough* when we want more of something.
- We use *too many* before something we can count. We use *too much* before something we can't count.

With nouns (e.g. *buses*, *information*)		
There are	too many	buses in this city.
	not enough	
There is	too much	information in this book.
	not enough	

With adjectives (e.g. *big*)			
This house is	too	big	.
	not		enough.

With verbs (e.g. *talk*)		
I don't	talk to my friends	enough.
I		too much.

It was too hot for me.

Present perfect for experience

- We use the present perfect to talk about our experiences. We form it with the present simple of the verb *have* + the past participle.
- We can form the negative with *have* + *not*, or use *never*.
- We often use *ever* in the question form to ask about someone's experiences in all their life.

I You We They	have	been to Brazil.
	haven't	
He She It	has	
	hasn't	

Have	I you we they	(ever)	been to Brazil?
Has	he she it		

Yes,	I you we they	have.
No,		haven't.
Yes,	he she it	has.
No,		hasn't.

Remember:
I have = I've   She has = She's
have not = haven't   has not = hasn't

We've won our match!

Present perfect with *just, already, yet*

- We often use the present perfect with the words *just*, *already* and *yet*.
- We use *just* to say that something happened a very short time ago. When we use it with the present perfect, it goes between the verb *have* and the past participle.

  Justin **has just started** at a new school, and he's feeling nervous.

- We use *already* to say that something happened before now. It usually also goes between the verb *have* and the past participle.

  I**'ve already been** to Japan twice, but I want to go back again next year.

- We use *not … yet* to say that something hasn't happened before now, and we use *yet* to ask questions. *Yet* usually comes at the end of a sentence.

  I **haven't learnt** the song **yet**. I'm going to do it this weekend.
  '**Have** you **learnt** the song **yet**?' 'No, I **haven't**.'

Jenny's just fallen off her camel!

Grammar reference

Past continuous

- We use the past continuous tense to talk about actions that continued for a period of time in the past. We form the past continuous tense with *was/were* and the *-ing* form of the verb (e.g. *doing*).

I He/She/It	was	watching a film.
You We They	were	

Was	I he/she/it	swimming in the pool?
Were	you we they	

Yes,	I he/she/it	was.
No,		wasn't.
Yes,	you we they	were.
No,		weren't.

- We often use the past continuous and the past simple together when one action interrupts another action.
  We **were eating** dinner when he **phoned** me.

He was driving slowly.

for and *since*

- We use the present perfect with *for* and *since* to talk about something that started in the past and continues into the present.
- We use *for* before a period of time (e.g. *five minutes, two weeks, three years*).
  Amy**'s lived** in this town **for** five years.
- We use *since* before the point in time when something started (e.g. *three o'clock, Friday, 2014*).
  Harry**'s been** at school **since** seven o'clock this morning.

will/won't

- We use *will* and *won't* to talk about actions and events in the future, and to make offers. We form it with *will/won't* and the base form of the verb (e.g. *do*).

I You He/She/It We They	'll	do the shopping.
	won't	

Will	I you he/she/it we they	do the shopping?
Won't		

Yes,	I you he/she/it we they	will.
No,		won't.

Remember:
I will = I'll   will not = won't

We'll have a lovely day out.

Conjunctions: *so* and *because*

- We use *so* and *because* to talk about the reasons why something happens. We use *because* to talk about causes. We use *so* to talk about effects.
- We often use a comma (,) before *so*, but we don't use one before *because*.

I'm not wearing my gloves,	→	**so** I've got cold hands.
I've got cold hands	→	**because** I'm not wearing my gloves.

Grammar reference 123

Tag questions

- We use tag questions at the end of a sentence to check that a statement is true. If the statement is positive, we usually use a negative tag question. If the statement is negative, we usually use a positive tag question. With most verbs in the present, we use *do/does* and *don't* in the question tag.

You **like** cycling,	→	don't you?
She **doesn't drink** coffee,	→	does she?

- When we're using the verb *to be*, an auxiliary verb (e.g. **are** going to do, **have** done) or a modal verb (e.g. *can, could, will*), we use those verbs in the question tag.

We **aren't** late,	→	are we?
He **is** going to the cinema tonight,	→	isn't he?
Jake **hasn't** done his homework,	→	has he?
Mia **can** ride a bike,	→	can't she?
They **couldn't** hear the music,	→	could they?
I **will** see you at the concert,	→	won't I?

That's the biggest robot in the world, isn't it?

- When the verb is in the past simple, we usually use *did* and *didn't* in the question tag. When we're using the verb *to be*, we use *was/were*.

We **went** to the same school, **didn't we**?
You **didn't see** the doctor, **did you**?
Charlie **wasn't** at home last night, **was he**?
The students **weren't** happy about the exam, **were they**?

Short questions

- We use short questions to show interest or surprise. We use a positive verb if the verb in the main sentence is positive. We use a negative verb if the verb in the main sentence is negative. Like tag questions, we use *do/does* and *don't* with most verbs in the present simple tense.

'Ella **lives** on this street.'	→	'Does she?'
'I **don't watch** TV in the morning.'	→	'Don't you?'

- If the main sentence uses the verb *to be*, an auxiliary verb (e.g. **are** going to do, **have** done) or a modal verb (e.g. *can, could, will*), we repeat it.

'Tom **is** a police officer.'	→	'Is he?'
'There **was** a fire at the factory last night.'	→	'Was there?'
'We **aren't** going to the concert tomorrow.'	→	'Aren't you?'
'I **have** lived here for three years.'	→	'Have you?'
'Emily **can** repair your bike.'	→	'Can she?'
'I **could** go to the shop for you.'	→	'Could you?'
'My brothers **will be** at the airport when we arrive tomorrow.'	→	'Will they?'

This puppy can play with a ball!

Can it?

Past participles

- We use past participles when we form the present perfect tense. For regular verbs, we form the past participle by adding -ed to the base form of the verb (e.g. *borrow – borrowed, start – started*).

  I've **borrowed** your tablet to play a game – I'll give it back!

  Harry has **started** playing the guitar, but it's quite difficult.

- There are a lot of irregular past participles (e.g. *forgot – forgotten, take – taken*). You can check the past participles of some important irregular verbs on p127.

  Josh has **forgotten** where he put his sports kit.

  My dad has **taken** thousands of photos on his camera; he's a photographer.

> I've hurt my leg a bit.

be used for/to

- We can use the phrases *be used for* and *be used to* to describe the purpose of an object. We use the -ing form of the verb after *be used for*. We use the base form of the verb (e.g. *do*) after *be used to*.

?	What **is** this machine **used for**?
+	This machine **is used for making** ice cream.
+	This machine **is used to make** ice cream.
+	100 years ago, candles **were used for lighting** people's homes.
+	In the past, animal skins **were used to write** on.

> Toothbrushes are used for cleaning your teeth.

will and going to

- We use *will* to say what we think will happen in the future (to make predictions). We form it with *will* or *won't* + the base form of the verb. (See p123 for a table with *will*.)

  In the future, we **won't drive** cars. They **will drive** themselves!

- We use *going to* to talk about our plans for the future. We form it with the verb *to be* + *going to* + the base form of the verb.

I	am 'm not	going to	eat lunch.
You We They	are aren't	going to	eat lunch.
He She	is isn't	going to	eat lunch.

Am	I	going to	eat lunch?
Are	you we they	going to	eat lunch?
Is	he she	going to	eat lunch?

> My astronaut is going to travel in an enormous spaceship.

Grammar reference

Review of past tenses

- We often use the past continuous and the past simple together when one action interrupts another action.

  We **were eating** dinner when he **phoned** me.

- The past simple describes the important, shorter action (*he phoned me*). The past continuous describes a longer action that happens before and after (*we were eating dinner*). We often use *when* before the verb in the past simple.

| I **was talking** to my friend on the phone | → | **when** I **heard** a loud noise outside. |
| Olivia and Nico **were watching** TV | → | **when** someone **knocked** on the door. |

It smells/tastes/looks/feels/sounds like …

- Verbs like *smell* and *taste* describe what we experience with our senses. We usually use adjectives after these verbs.

  Lily's trainers **smell** bad because she wore them in the rain.

- We use verbs like *smell* and *taste* with *like* to say what something is similar to or what something might be. We use a noun after *like*.

Dad's socks	**smell like**	old cheese.
This bread	**tastes like**	the bread we ate in Italy.
That cloud	**looks like**	a plane.
This jumper	**feels like**	wool.
That noise	**sounds like**	my phone.

They look like spaghetti, but they don't taste like spaghetti.

Make somebody + adjective

- We use *make somebody* + adjective to talk about how a person feels as a result of something. We form it with the verb *to make* + object (e.g. *me, you*) + adjective.

| Loud music | **makes** | me/you/him/her/us/them | angry. |
| Long queues | **make** | | |

Unit 9

Grammar reference

Irregular verb list

Base form	Past simple	Past participle
be	was/were	been
begin	began	begun
break	broke	broken
bring	brought	brought
build	built	built
buy	bought	bought
can	could	been able
catch	caught	caught
choose	chose	chosen
come	came	come
cut	cut	cut
do	did	done
draw	drew	drawn
drink	drank	drunk
drive	drove	driven
eat	ate	eaten
fall	fell	fallen
feed	fed	fed
feel	felt	felt
find	found	found
fly	flew	flown
forget	forgot	forgotten
get	got	got
give	gave	given
go	went	gone
grow	grew	grown
have	had	had
hear	heard	heard
hide	hid	hidden
hit	hit	hit
hold	held	held
hurt	hurt	hurt
keep	kept	kept
know	knew	known
learn	learnt	learnt
leave	left	left

Base form	Past simple	Past participle
let	let	let
lie	lay	lain
lose	lost	lost
make	made	made
mean	meant	meant
meet	met	met
put	put	put
read	read	read
ride	rode	ridden
run	ran	run
say	said	said
see	saw	seen
sell	sold	sold
send	sent	sent
sing	sang	sung
sit	sat	sat
sleep	slept	slept
smell	smelt	smelt
speak	spoke	spoken
spell	spelt	spelt
spend	spent	spent
stand	stood	stood
steal	stole	stolen
swim	swam	swum
swing	swung	swung
take	took	taken
teach	taught	taught
tell	told	told
think	thought	thought
throw	threw	thrown
understand	understood	understood
wake	woke	woken
wear	wore	worn
win	won	won
write	wrote	written